Moscow Coup

MOSCOW COUP
The Death of the Soviet System

Martin Sixsmith

S I M O N & S C H U S T E R

LONDON·SYDNEY·NEW YORK·TOKYO·SINGAPORE·TORONTO

First published in Great Britain by
Simon & Schuster Ltd in 1991
A Paramount Communications Company

Copyright © Martin Sixsmith, 1991

Simon & Schuster Ltd
West Garden Place
Kendal Street
London W2 2AQ

Simon & Schuster of Australia Pty Ltd
Sydney

A CIP catalouge record for this book is
available from the British Library
ISBN 0–671–71124–5

Typeset in Bembo 11 on 13 with Rockwell by
Falcon Typographic Art Ltd, Edinburgh & London
Printed and bound in Great Britain by
Butler & Tanner Ltd, Frome

Contents

Introduction

Blessed is he who visits this earth
At it moments of destiny.
Fyodor Tyutchev (1803–73)

On 19 August 1991 all who were present in Moscow knew with absolute certainty that history was being made and unmade before our eyes.

When the tanks and armoured vehicles chased the usual Moskviches and Ladas from the streets of the capital, churning up the asphalt and crunching the kerb stones, they left an indelible mark not only on the face of the city, but on the course of Soviet and world history: the failed August coup in the Soviet Union will almost certainly be remembered as the single most significant event of the second half of the twentieth century.

There is no denying that the coup took us by surprise. Even two years spent in Poland at the culmination of the Solidarity revolution had done little to prepare me for what eventually transpired in the Soviet Union. In Poland, Communism was an imported, alien creed which the people had struggled against for decades. The memory of the inter-war years, when Poland and much of eastern Europe enjoyed a semblance of democracy and a market economy that encouraged the values of enterprise and independent thought, made it seem natural for truly representative political forces to arise and throw off the Communist yoke. In eastern Europe, the revolutions of the late 1980s were a return to a status quo which had been temporarily displaced by a foreign aberration. The discredited Communist leaders were naturally replaced by a new generation of politicians, untainted by the old regime, many of whom had served their political apprenticeship in Communist jails or operating clandestinely as an underground opposition.

But in the Soviet Union there was none of this. Communism as a political goal had been introduced not by a foreign power but by native forces, led by a man who for seventy years was worshipped and prayed to by generations. If Lenin had taken on the role of God, Communism (or the aspiration to Communism) had literally become the state. Since the Bolsheviks outlawed other political groupings in the wake of the 1917 revolution, no organized opposition had ever surfaced. Political change was only possible from within the ranks of the Communist party; but even more than that, the party controlled every aspect of life in the Soviet Union. Through its system of nomenklatura, every appointment of every public official however high or low was either made directly by party committees or was subject to approval by party bodies with the right of veto. The party controlled the army and police, but it also controlled factory managers, teachers, journalists and anyone else who could have the slightest influence on public life. There was no effective political opposition either underground or above ground; and in the face of ruthless suppression by the state, the scattered dissident groups could manage little more than a sporadic monitoring of the human rights abuses they and others were subjected to.

In such an atmosphere, aspiring politicians – even those who may initially have wanted to change the system – went inevitably into the Communist party; and the party's pervasive moulding, its intolerance of disagreement and its subjugation of recruits from the earliest age to its distorted set of social values meant that no generation of untainted leaders existed or could exist. There were no Vaclav Havels or Lech Walesas waiting in the wings for their chance to take on the mantle of power. Boris Yeltsin was a card carrying Communist until 12 July 1990; Mikhail Gorbachov would still be one if he had not been pushed into disbanding the party by the August events. Radicals like mayors Anatoly Sobchak of Leningrad and Gavriil Popov of Moscow were still Communists a year before the coup; and Eduard Shevardnadze is remembered as a cruel and repressive party boss from the days of his early political career in his native Georgia. (Even the few former political prisoners who have now inherited some measure of power – notably the fanatical president of Georgia, Zviad Gamsakhurdia – have found it difficult to escape the clutches of the political culture imposed by the Communists: Gamsakhurdia the Georgian nationalist has shown himself to be equally, or more, intolerant and dictatorial than those who held the post before him.) Perhaps the greatest tragedy of modern Soviet politics is that Andrei Sakharov, one of the few who managed to maintain his integrity and still wield influence in the Soviet Union, should have died as the ideals he espoused were on the threshold of being realized.

In such conditions, there had been few grounds for expecting any fundamental changes in the political structure of the Soviet Union, let alone the revolution which occurred in August. Even the Soviet people had long seemed resigned to the system they had been born to. From many, there was genuine pride in a political creed which was, after all, of their own making, which had defeated the monster of right-wing German tyranny in 1945, and which had turned their country into a military if not an industrial superpower. From millions more, there was a tacit acceptance that the regime was too powerful to challenge and that the business of simply getting on with life under difficult conditions precluded the luxury of even contemplating any attempt to fight the system. Finally, from those who had benefited under Communism – the bureaucrats, the managers, the local officials and even the ordinary folk who knew the party would keep their children out of college if they rocked the boat – there was a concerted desire to keep the system in place, to strengthen the hand that could feed them favours and advancement.

Most of all, there was the deep rooted feeling that the Russian people – and those of the empire that Russia had gathered unto itself – had no memory, no understanding, nor even any desire to understand the realities of political freedom. Seventy years of Communist totalitarianism had been merely a continuation of a centuries old tradition: the totalitarianism of the tsars stretched right back to the totalitarianism of the Tatars, who consolidated the concept in Russia in the thirteenth century. At no time since then had Russians enjoyed more than a tentative flowering of liberty, democracy or self-determination, and every attempt to introduce such alien ideas had met with rapid and ignominious defeat. (There are many who argue that the country is simply unsuited to such a system and would perish if it were introduced in any concerted form.)

All the omens, then, were discouraging. How could fundamental change take place in a society where everything was against it? How could a Communist party which controlled the very fabric of society, and which could crush any embryonic challenges to its authority by calling on the forces of repression it wielded with impunity, suddenly lose power? How could it so conclusively fall from grace as to be banned in the country it once bestrode? How could it allow the empire which had been painstakingly gathered over the course of centuries to collapse and fall apart?

The answer is one which would appeal to a Marxist with a sense of humour: the August events were, in essence, the result of an unstoppable historical process which has swept the globe, and which has finally spread even to a country that has doggedly tried to keep the dialectical blinds drawn against the world. The age of empire is over – Britain, France and others discovered it long ago – and only the Soviets were holding out against the trend. The age of enlightenment, political activism, and demand for liberation from oppressive ideologies had reached fruition, and only the Soviets were trying to deny it. The economic triumph of free market capitalism – with all its drawbacks and imperfections – had become so abundantly clear that only the Soviet Union's most blinkered ideologues were continuing to argue with it. The days when Khrushchev could boast of his intention to 'bury the West' (economically speaking) and not draw a guffaw, when the call to 'catch up with and overtake America' could still be taken seriously, were long gone.

But if history's long game was running against the Communists, that did not mean that the August revolution was any the less unexpected. The flaw of the dialectical reading of history is that it almost always needs hindsight to predict a future which it smoothly claims was inevitable. There were, though, signs which might have made us greet the events of summer 1991 with a little less astonishment, and it will be part of this book's task to try to trace the key developments which led up to them. The process of perestroika had, after all, been in progress for more than six years. Its early stages had been painfully slow and it had suffered set back after set back, but Gorbachov was undeniably changing Soviet society. How, though, to explain the speed with which the seemingly impregnable Communist system allowed itself to be swept away?

The outstanding historian of the French and American revolutions, Alexis de Tocqueville, posited the now well-thumbed concept that 'an authoritarian regime faces the greatest moment of danger when it begins to reform itself'. The theory is, essentially, that a regime – however small its power base and however much it is hated – can stay in power if it continues to convince its subjects that there is no chance for them to remove it. Once it starts to offer reforms – however slight, or however much the regime may wish to control the pace of change – it immediately destroys the confidence trick which had previously maintained its well being. Once the people are aware that the regime is not infallible, once they see that change is after all possible, they will unfailingly begin to demand greater and more rapid reforms until the whole edifice of power crumbles.

That, to a certain extent, is what happened in the Soviet Union. The Communist party was, to all intents and purposes, so entrenched that it could only be dislodged if the party itself began to undermine its own authority, and Gorbachov was the man to do that. Like de Tocqueville's historical autocrats, he began his reform of the system with only small changes in mind. (He was, essentially, forced into tinkering with the status quo because of the critical state of the Soviet economy, and the realization that something had to be changed or the whole country would sink into economic collapse.) In the early years of perestroika Gorbachov hoped he could lead the reforms from the top, dictating the pace of change and ensuring that things did not run out of control. But, like de Tocqueville's historical masses, the Soviet people stepped forward to play their part in the theorem, sensing that change was afoot and demanding more of it. Perestroika began to be led from below, not from above; and it was the people – with new potential leaders they picked up along the way – who began to call the shots.

So far, so good. But the final surge of aggression from a long cowed people, from a nation which had previously bowed its head to all the iniquities of an oppressive system, was nonetheless a surprise and a revelation. The will to resist the tanks during that week in August was the expression of a human spirit which had lain dormant in the Soviet people, but which had never – through all the trials it was subjected to – been crushed. The people resisted the tanks because they knew instinctively it was right to do so, and that moment marked the rebirth of a long submerged natural dignity in the Soviet Union. All the decades of Communist cant and distortion had not destroyed the basic human sense of morality. And in the short term it was Gorbachov himself who had given them the knowledge they needed to fight off the coup: instead of blindly obeying the men who controlled the traditional instruments of power, his years of perestroika had awakened the people's will to think for themselves and to fight for what is right.

In the end Gorbachov was correct when he said the defeat of the coup was due to values he himself had taught, but that in itself was not enough to save him from a personal reversal which has ended his days as the leading political force in the country. Like so many east European leaders who opened the flood gates to reform, Gorbachov seems on the point of being swept away by the powerful currents he himself unleashed, too weighed down by his connections with the old system, and too slow to adapt to the new realities, to swim at the head of the new tide of change.

The initial euphoria over the collapse of Soviet Communism has quickly given way to doubt and anxiety over what is likely to replace it, and the second task of this book is to try to look forward to the consequences the August coup may have for the new, tentatively named Union of Sovereign States. Russia has followed the lead taken by Spain and Portugal in the 1970s and repeated in eastern Europe a decade later: at a moment when the forces of extreme reaction were poised to take power, to try to lead the country back towards its own past, and when supporters of that course had shown themselves ready to use violence in its furtherance, the people have shown the courage to say No. But that stand in the cause of self-determination and social justice is, of itself, no lasting guarantee of future democracy. The ghosts of the Iranian revolution which overthrew the Shah only for him to be replaced by Ayatollah Khomeini, or Nicaragua which swapped Somoza for the Sandinistas, may yet return to haunt Russia.

That, though, is for the future. For the moment our subject is the spectacular overthrow of the political system which wrought the most far reaching changes of twentieth century thought, which conquered half the globe and threatened to conquer the other half, but which ended its days ignominiously on the streets of Moscow . . . the end of Communism in a moment of destiny for the whole world.

PART 1

The Drama

1

Monday, 19 August

The first indication that things were badly wrong that Monday morning was the solemn music that Soviet TV was putting out in place of its usual early morning news and chat show. A quick check on the radio revealed all channels broadcasting the same composers – Tchaikovsky and Chopin: the classical harbingers of grave news in the Soviet Union. A growing sense of panic was briefly relieved by a glance through the curtains to the street below: there, people were still going about their business, the usual militiaman was on guard duty outside the front entrance of the flats opposite and cars were heading down the main road into the city centre. But the relief was only momentary. The strains of 'Swan Lake' were unceremoniously interrupted, and a funereal sounding announcer made the proclamation that was to chill the hearts of millions:

> In connection with Mikhail Gorbachov's inability to carry out his duties of President due to reasons of ill health and in accordance with article 127 of the Soviet Constitution, all presidential powers have been transferred to the Vice-President of the USSR, Gennady Yanayev.

For any Russian listening, the situation was already clear: retirement for health reasons was the cynical old formula that had been used for decades to remove public officials unwillingly from their posts. But in case there was any doubt left that a coup was in progress, the announcement went on to spell it out:

> With the aim of overcoming the deep crisis, political, inter-ethnic and civil confrontation, chaos and anarchy which are threatening the life and safety of citizens of the Soviet Union, as well as the sovereignty, integrity, freedom and independence of our fatherland, we the undersigned hereby announce . . . the introduction of a state of emergency in parts of the USSR for a period of six months beginning on 19 August at 4 a.m. Moscow time . . . and the setting up of a State Emergency Committee to run the country and effectively administer the emergency regime.

The list of signatories left little doubt about the nature of the new regime. It was headed by Yanayev, and included all the hardliners from the top Kremlin leadership – Vladimir Kryuchkov, head of the KGB; Valentin Pavlov, the conservative Prime Minister; Boris Pugo, the Interior Minister who controlled the militia and forces of special troops; and Defence Minister, Marshal Dmitri Yazov. These were the men who for months had been expressing growing irritation with the way things were going in the Soviet Union, not overtly criticizing Mikhail Gorbachov, but making plain their belief that reform had gone far enough and that it was time to reintroduce a little law and order.

Things were beginning to fall into place. Just two days earlier Gorbachov's old liberal ally Aleksandr Yakovlev had been expelled from the Communist movement for advocating the creation of a new political party based on respect for democracy and reform. He had clearly taken his expulsion badly, and when he called a small group of journalists into his office to share his thoughts he was visibly shaken and shaking. At first, we put this down to the emotion of his break with a party he had served for decades. He was, it seemed, bitter that Gorbachov had done nothing to help him; but he went on to suggest that the cause of his distress was much more serious. There was, said Yakovlev, a neo-stalinist clique which had gained control of the Communist party leadership and was preparing a move to destroy all the gains of perestroika and glasnost.

This was on the Saturday before the coup and Yakovlev would give no source to substantiate his allegations. Neither would he name the men he believed were behind the putative plot (although his bitterness against Gorbachov and his insistence that he could never be reconciled with the Soviet leader took on increased resonance in light of later suggestions that Gorbachov himself may have stage managed the coup.)

At the time we reported Yakovlev's warnings, but subsequent events proved that we failed to give them adequate credence. Eduard Shevardnaze's dramatic resignation speech in December 1990, in which he warned of impending dictatorship, was followed a month later by the failed military putsch in Lithuania and Latvia. Aleksandr Yakovlev's predictions took only two days to come true, with consequences that were much more far-reaching.

By 10 a.m. on that Monday morning it was clear that this was a hardline putsch by men who would be doing their utmost to return the USSR to its old, orthodox-Communist past. But the question immediately arose of how they intended to enforce their authority. Gorbachov would almost certainly be under arrest, but what about all the radical politicians who were the natural opponents of the new regime? Would they also be rounded up? Would there be tanks on the streets?

A hasty drive around Moscow's main ring-road produced no evidence of any unusual military activity. The picture was the same down at the Kremlin and on Red Square. So was this a coup only in words, or were the strong-arm tactics about to begin?

The question was answered thirty minutes later when the first column of tanks swept into sight down Kutuzovsky Prospekt, the broad avenue where Leonid Brezhnev used to have his apartment: the thought was irresistible that if the old dictator could have seen the view from his window now, he would have applauded. And the convoy continued, mostly light armoured vehicles and armoured personnel carriers, rolling now down Kalinin Prospekt and on towards the Kremlin.

In the first hours of Monday morning there was initially little reaction from Moscovites on the streets: few of them could have fully realized what was happening. Resistance began only later in the day. We followed the armour and there was no attempt by the military to ward us off. Their main concern seemed to be one of the tanks which had broken down in the middle of the avenue and was holding up the rest of the column. It seemed like a scene from the endless rehearsals for the Revolution Day parades we had witnessed over the years, but this time the tanks were preparing not for a triumphant roll through Red Square, but for possible action in a battle which threatened to pit Russian against Russian.

As we watched the military pieces being moved into place, a new announcement on the car radio brought us further clarification of the political equation that was taking shape. The coup leaders were now attempting to explain and justify their actions in a lengthy appeal to the Soviet nation. For the first time the hardliners were able to do openly what they had always shrunk from doing in the past, and a stream of invective against Mikhail Gorbachov was unleashed on the airwaves. 'Our motherland is in mortal danger,' said the appeal. 'The policy of reform begun by M. Gorbachov has run into a dead end. . . . The existing authorities have lost the trust of the people. Political manoeuvring has destroyed any concern about the fate of the fatherland. All institutions of the State are openly mocked. The country has become ungovernable.'

There followed a lengthy exposé of all the noxious effects which Gorbachov's years in power had brought for the country: ethnic conflicts causing hundreds of deaths and hundreds of thousands of refugees; screeds of empty words from the Gorbachov administration masking a total lack of positive action; a chaotic and uncoordinated transition to a market economy which unleashed profiteering, economic collapse and plunging standards of living; a growing popular discontent which was threatening to spill over into widespread unrest; an irresponsible reliance on help from the capitalist West; growing unemployment, crime and lawlessness.

On Gorbachov's foreign policy record, the hardliners were particularly indignant: he had, they said, undermined the Soviet Union's standing in the world to the point where foreign powers were beginning to take control of the nation's destiny, where a Soviet citizen who yesterday felt proud of his nationality was now regarded as a second-class being. The announcement pledged that the new rulers of the Soviet Union would restore the country to its rightful place of pride and honour – an appeal to the sense of patriotism felt by many Russians to have been offended by Gorbachov's subservience to the West.

All in all, it was a blinkered and xenophobic approach which bode ill for Moscow's partners in the world community. A second appeal by the coup leaders, this time to the United Nations and foreign heads of state, sought to calm fears abroad that the USSR under new management was moving back towards cold war policies of confrontation. The Soviet Union, it said, would remain peace-loving and committed to uphold all the international obligations it had entered into – an assurance which carried little weight in light of the known views of its signatories. Men like Dmitri Yazov and Boris Pugo, who had never had much respect for arms reduction treaties which slashed the forces under their command and who had done their utmost to sabotage the CFE accord reducing conventional forces in Europe, were unlikely to have undergone a sudden conversion to the ideals of disarmament and rapprochement with the capitalist enemy.

One man whose name did not appear at the end of all the official statements – who was not even officially a member of the eight man Emergency Committee – was Anatoly Lukyanov, the speaker of the Supreme Soviet (the country's standing parliament). He was a university friend of Mikhail Gorbachov – they had known each other for forty years – but the talk of the streets was that the *eminence grise* behind the coup, the man pulling the strings but keeping out of public sight, was none other than Lukyanov himself. This view was later confirmed by investigations into the genesis of the plot and Lukyanov was arraigned on treason charges, along with the others who played a more open role. On 19 August, though, his only visible contribution to the takeover was to block moves for an emergency session of parliament. Despite repeated demands from radical deputies for an emergency sitting – which might have allowed liberal condemnation of the coup to be made public – Lukyanov was unyielding: the earliest date he would even consider was 26 August, a week later, by which time the plotters clearly hoped to be so firmly entrenched that no amount of parliamentary opposition would ever unseat them. By barring the Supreme Soviet from meeting, Lukyanov effectively prevented it from playing the central resistance role which the Russian parliament was already taking on. When accounts were finally settled after the coup, the Supreme Soviet itself was severely attacked for its lack of courage compared to the decisiveness and bravery of the Russian parliament.

By mid-day on Monday, one of the first signs of passive resistance to the coup had emerged in the changing voices of the news readers who were forced to declaim the plotters' propaganda. From an emotionless beginning, tones of disgust with the material they were reading slowly began to appear: one woman announcer could hardly disguise her contempt, and her feelings showed more and more clearly in her voice. The plotters were seemingly finding it hard to find supporters of their views in key positions.

Physical resistance was also about to begin on the streets. Reports were coming in of isolated incidents in which civilians had stood in the path of advancing tanks, hurling abuse at the troops or appealing to them to go back to barracks. There was one particularly dramatic incident in which demonstrators clambered onto an armoured personnel carrier and began to drag the driver out of his porthole: the look of terror on the face of the teenaged conscript at the threat of a public beating suggested that some of the troops at least might not be spoiling for a fight. Many of the tank crews had seemed unsure how to respond. Few of them had any idea why they had been ordered onto the streets of Moscow, but nearly all of those we spoke to said they would obey whatever orders they were given.

So far, caution and good sense shown by the tank commanders had averted any injuries to those who stood in their way: when challenged, the tanks simply wheeled around the human obstacles in their path and took another route to their destination. A feeling of impunity began to grow in those who were bold enough to oppose the army. A persistent rumour began to circulate that the troops were not armed, or that their guns were unloaded. But when we asked several squaddies riding on the back of armoured personnel carriers whether this was true, they denied it. One tank commander showed me the shells he had ready to fire from his main cannon, and the live rounds loaded in his soldiers' rifles – weaponry that was destined to kill at least three civilians the following day.

By Monday afternoon the army was everywhere and the worst fears of supporters of democracy had been realized. The men who claimed to have taken power in the Soviet Union were showing their true face, relying not on the ballot box but on the bullet. Columns of armoured vehicles surrounded strategic buildings in Moscow, meeting resistance from the people, resistance that was still largely token, but which was enough to hint at the violence and bloodshed which more organized opposition seemed certain to provoke.

In mid afternoon a phalanx of the heaviest tanks drew up outside the Russian parliament on the banks of the Moskva river. This was the headquarters of Boris Yeltsin, the Russian President whose outspoken support of radical reform had made him the natural rallying point for resistance to the coup. As soon as the takeover was announced in the early hours of Monday morning, Yeltsin had gathered his trusted aides and taken refuge in the parliament, a soaring white marble building whose nickname of Belyi Dom – the White House – quickly made it a nationally and internationally recognized symbol of democracy. It was here that the fight for the democratic ideal in the Soviet Union was to be fought out over the next two days and nights.

When the tanks arrived, belching acrid fumes and smoke, thundering noisily along the embankment and leaving the deep imprint of their tracks in the tarmac, Yeltsin was inside the building trying to formulate a response to the coup. The parliament was undefended, there were no crowds present and the building was seemingly ripe for the taking. I watched the line of armour draw up at the base of the parliament steps and was convinced they had come to seize the parliament, Boris Yeltsin and all who opposed their masters in the Kremlin.

For twenty minutes the tanks stayed in place, revving their engines and filling the air with a blue haze. But the order to attack did not come, and at the crucial moment it was Yeltsin himself who seized the initiative. Instead of waiting for the troops to come for him, Yeltsin went to the troops. Emerging dramatically from the parliament's main entrance, Yeltsin descended the steps and strode confidently towards the leading tank in the column.

For a moment, all who were present held their breath. Yeltsin was accompanied by his usual bodyguards, but there was no one to save him from a concerted attempt to arrest him, nothing to save him from a sniper's bullet. It seemed then that the one man who could stand in the way of the coup, the one man on whose shoulders the future of Russian democracy had come to rest, was gambling everything on a confrontation he could have avoided. Yeltsin could have stayed safely inside the parliament, kept his head down and waited. But patience was never Yeltsin's strong point and his decision to go for broke was to pay quick dividends.

In a master stroke of public image-making, he heaved his burly frame firmly onto the back of the tank he had selected, and then squarely onto the turret itself. Panting from the effort, he leaned down, shook hands with two startled tank crew who were peering from inside the vehicle, and then rose to his full height. Staring defiantly at the soldiers and militia around him, he declared to all within earshot that the army was with the people, that the troops would not attack the defenders of democracy and that the plotters in the Kremlin were doomed to failure. Right across Russia, said Yeltsin, workers were heeding his appeals for protest strikes and were walking out to show their opposition to the coup.

It was a performance of genius which set the tone for the whole of the resistance campaign in the coming hours and days. But Yeltsin could have felt very little conviction in anything he was saying. There had, presumably, been some secret agreement reached between Yeltsin's representatives and the tank commanders that he would not be shot or arrested if he came out to speak to them. But there was no record of what passed between Yeltsin and the tank crew in that moment of high drama, there was almost certainly no pledge of loyalty from the army despite Yeltsin's claims, and the next twenty-four hours showed that a large proportion of the armed forces were indeed ready to follow orders issued by the Kremlin, and were not even contemplating switching sides. Yeltsin's appeal for strikes, far from being heeded across the land, had probably gone unheard by the vast majority of workers: all his means of communication, including his access to national radio and newspapers, had been effectively cut off by the coup leaders, and whatever statements he made reached little further than those who could hear the hastily installed public address system outside the Russian parliament.

But, showing himself a man with his ear to the flow of history, Yeltsin on the turret of the tank had seized the genuine mood of the time. Some of the army was indeed wavering in its loyalties, and Yeltsin's intention was to encourage that indecision by suggesting it was more widespread than it really was – the effects were seen later, when a parachute detachment and some tanks did in fact come to help defend the parliament. Similarly, his contention that workers were striking in their thousands was intended to stir up protests against the coup, protests which did eventually begin to materialize.

On the basis of what he knew at the time, though, Yeltsin had no objective grounds for feeling the optimism he professed. It was, it seems, an inspired piece of whistling in the dark; but in the immediate term it did the trick. Shortly after Yeltsin descended from his perch to go back to his parliament under siege, the tank commanders conferred briefly, jumped back on board and the tanks roared off along the embankment leaving the parliament once again in peace.

It is unclear whether the initiative came from the commanders themselves, or whether their original orders had been simply to intimidate Yeltsin and then leave, but the effect on those present was electrifying. Yeltsin had stood up to the tanks and won – a precious psychological victory at a time when the coup looked almost certain to succeed.

The full resonance of the tank episode was confirmed later that day, when the poet Yevgeny Yevtushenko called at the BBC office with a new poem he had written celebrating Yeltsin's appearance. In Russia, poetry is written and read with burning commitment: long-standing restrictions on other means of expression have made it an accepted medium of political struggle and the written word can still fall like a bombshell. Yevtushenko had brought with him his Russian text and a rough English translation with the intention of broadcasting it to the world. For an hour or more we sat over the poem, polishing it and correcting some of his more idiosyncratic uses of English. Entitled 'August 19th', it summed up the feeling that we were living an historic moment and that Yeltsin's courage might just be enough to bring the nation through its torment:

> This August day
> Shall be glorified in songs and ballads.
> Today we are a nation,
> No longer fools, happy to be fooled . . .
> Conscience wakens even in the tanks –
> Yeltsin rises on a turret,
> Freed from ghosts of Kremlin leaders past . . .

On that Monday Yevtushenko's optimism was still little more than hopeful prescience. Around the city the army was tightening its grip. At the headquarters of Soviet television the troops had been in place since early morning, barring the way to journalists and technicians arriving for work: the army commander had a list of television personnel considered 'reliable', and only they were admitted to the building. In truth, only a skeleton staff was needed for the purposes Yanayev and his men had in mind: normal programming was suspended, and all that was really needed was someone to change the Tchaikovsky tapes from time to time. There were, though, enough journalists willing to sell their souls to enable the plotters to put together so-called news bulletins, which in reality were little more than recitations of official statements and propaganda. It was a test of honour for those working in the media – some passed with flying colours, others caved in and compromised themselves in return for a few favours from the Kremlin.

At the television and radio tower in the suburb of Ostankino, there were similar scenes. Tanks had been drawn up around the base of the tower and all transmission capacity brought under the control of the regime (although satellite links for foreign TV companies were never cut, presumably reflecting Yanayev's residual fear of antagonizing the West: it was the first example of a lack of consistency or of courage by the putschists which was to characterize many aspects of their conduct in the coming days).

The plotters were obsessed with shutting down the domestic media. It was the old Soviet reaction to seize control of sources of information, and it looked like signalling a definitive end to the brief flowering of glasnost. In the circumstances it was a policy which seemed well founded: under Gorbachov, newspapers and broadcasters had begun to speak with an independent voice, even though Gorbachov himself had recently begun the process of reining back the media freedoms he had earlier initiated. (His appointment of the lugubrious Leonid Kravchuk as Head of State Broadcasting several months previously had resulted in the banning of the most outspoken news and current affairs programmes, an incursion into glasnost which was only partially made good by the development of television's Second Programme run by Yeltsin's Russian Federation and largely reflecting his views.)

The result of the media clamp-down was that the overwhelming majority of Soviets had no access to unbiased information about events in Moscow and the other major cities. They simply did not know that tanks were on the streets; they did not know that resistance was building around the Russian parliament; and if the coup had succeeded, they would probably have never known the truth of what occurred in the capital. It would have been the victors who wrote the history of the times, and past experience of Bolshevik manipulations suggested that the coup leaders would have written it in a way which reflected only their point of view.

A new decree by the State Emergency Committee, made public in mid-afternoon, also banned all newspapers and magazines except for nine specified publications. These consisted, not surprisingly, of hardline dailies like *Pravda*, *Sovietskaya Rossiya*, *Trud* (the trades union paper) and *Krasnaya Zvezda* (the army journal). The only unexpected inclusion was *Izvestiya*, still officially the government newspaper, but increasingly liberal in tone since the reign of its former editor Ivan Laptev. His legacy had been undermined in the weeks before the coup by the appointment of hardliners to key editorial positions, and the man behind those appointments, Supreme Soviet chairman Anatoly Lukyanov – now deeply implicated in the staging of the coup – presumably felt that the gagging measures he had imposed would be enough to make *Izvestiya* toe the line.

But Lukyanov had reckoned without the determination and integrity of some of the journalists working on the paper. Faced with an ultimatum to print the news as determined by the politicians, the journalists revolted. The key battle came as section editors and reporters demanded the right to print Yeltsin's point of view as well as that of Yanayev and his cronies. With the printers also backing the journalists, a compromise was eventually reached which allowed Yeltsin's condemnation of the coup and his call for a general strike to appear on an inside page. The *Izvestiya* staff had struck at least one blow for freedom of expression, which allowed the voice of resistance to be heard that Monday, when the evening editions – in much reduced numbers – hit the news-stands. It was a small victory, but compared with the cowardice and self-serving compliance of virtually all the other papers (*Pravda* in particular sold out shamelessly to the plotters), it was a shining example.

Other traditionally radical publications were simply closed down and their offices sealed, although *Moscow News* did manage to bring out a couple of broadsheet, single page editions using very basic equipment and photocopying machines located in journalists' flats and other secret locations. To many of us, the scenes in these apartments-cum-printing works brought back bitter memories of the old days of dissident samizdat publishing, when the truth was forced underground and could only be found in hand-distributed, cyclostyled sheets of nearly illegible print.

By the early hours of Monday afternoon, though, our short-wave receivers were picking up a new voice: a faint, sometimes inaudible signal had appeared on the airwaves, giving a very different interpretation of events from that in the official media. The station identified itself as the voice of the Russian people, saying it was broadcasting from a clandestine transmitter inside the Russian parliament. This was – at last – the outlet Boris Yeltsin had been seeking since his All-Russian TV channel and Radio Russia had been closed down during the night. The crackly broadcasts called for resistance to the coup, giving detailed information about tank movements in Moscow, and bringing the first reliable details of what was happening in other cities around the country. (We were relieved to hear that troops had not moved into Leningrad, but depressed that other republics seemed to be acquiescing in the takeover.)

The signal from Yeltsin's headquarters was weak and only those with short-wave sets could receive it (short-wave radios, which had traditionally been used to listen to the BBC Russian Service and Voice of America had gone out of fashion during the glasnost years, because information was more freely available from the domestic media), but the fact that the media blockade was being breached in even a small way was encouragement enough. It was only when we visited the radio station's premises in the Russian parliament that we realized how difficult their operating conditions were: their studio was little more than a broom cupboard with an ancient microphone and a few wires leading to a makeshift transmitter on the roof of the building.

At four in the afternoon, with troops now controlling all key installations in the city, the first signs of organized resistance emerged. Several hundred supporters of Boris Yeltsin gathered in Manezhnaya

Square under the shadow of the Kremlin walls. Their very presence was in itself an act of defiance, because the regime had just issued a decree banning demonstrations and calling for the police and army to ensure no illegal gatherings took place. The demonstrators chanted 'No to Fascism' and 'Down with the red junta', waving the tricoloured flag of pre-revolutionary, non-Communist Russia which had been adopted as the symbol of Yeltsin's pro-democracy campaign. The slogans were all in support of Boris Yeltsin, but the demonstrators took their cue from Yeltsin himself in calling for the reinstatement of the legal government and Mikhail Gorbachov. After years of feuding and personal hatred, the crisis facing the country had forged an alliance in extremis between the two men whose visions of democracy differed in detail but coincided on the main issue: tyranny must never be allowed to return. For the moment, Yeltsin and Gorbachov were united, but neither was in a position to act, and there was no guarantee that their alliance would last any longer than the crisis itself.

It was fortunate for the demonstrators that the security forces did not enforce their orders from the Kremlin with any greater vigour. Rows of army trucks carrying troops in riot gear had formed up in side streets around Manezhnaya Square, enough to crush the illegal demonstration in minutes, but the order to move in wasn't given and in the end the demonstrators dispersed of their own accord, knowing that the military's forbearance now might not be repeated in the future. It was widely reported that the army commanders had warned hospitals and clinics to expect the arrival of a large number of casualties.

By now, the classic images of military putsches from eastern Europe's past were being recreated all over the city: like the Czech students in 1968 or the Hungarian revolutionaries of 1956, Moscovites were throwing themselves in the path of advancing tanks, or clambering onto the guns to try to stop the assault on democracy. On the bridge leading up to the Soviet Foreign Ministry, I saw one elderly woman stand in front of an armoured personnel carrier and appeal to the soldiers to shoot her: she said she didn't want to live in a country where the ideals and freedoms she had fought for and had at last seen realized were now about to be crushed. It was only through a combination of good fortune and good sense from most of the tank commanders that injuries were largely avoided at this stage.

The ghosts of Prague and Budapest were present in more than just the street images: it was clear that what was happening in Moscow was also a repetition of the political drama that had been fought out in eastern Europe in the past. These were again the tanks of orthodox Marxism coming to rescue the socialist ideal from a reformist regime which had violated its purity; the Kremlin was again invoking the Brezhnev doctrine which allowed the use of force in the defence of Communism. But this time the democratizing enemy was not hundreds of miles away in a foreign land: it was here in the very heart of Moscow, a reformist cancer which had to be weeded out of the home of Communism itself. Gorbachov was the enemy; Yeltsin was the enemy; the Soviet people who wanted freedom and self-determination were the enemy. Yanayev and his men were saviours who would rescue the nation from itself.

In 1968 in Prague and in 1956 in Budapest, the Red Army had not hesitated to do its duty, with tragic and bloody consequences. In 1991 there was little to suggest the military would act any differently. In an unintentional but chilling echo, they had even chosen the third week in August to mount their putsch, just as they had done in Czechoslovakia twenty three years earlier. There was only the hope that times had changed, that six years of perestroika might have instilled a sense of responsibility and choice into the army commanders, and most of all there was the fact that the people the troops might be called upon to slaughter were themselves Russians.

In the early evening of Monday, the battle lines for an impending showdown had been drawn on the streets and were about to be drawn in the corridors of power too. From the Russian parliament, Boris Yeltsin issued a final challenge to the men in the Kremlin: the Yanayev regime, said Yeltsin, was illegal and its decrees must be disobeyed. All the orders of the State Emergency Committee were hereby revoked on the territory of the Russian Federation and any official carrying out such orders would himself be subject to prosecution.

But all Yeltsin's threats – and he himself was aware of this – carried little real weight. He was a prisoner in his own parliament, unable to act or to enforce his own rulings, and the officials he was threatening were the last people he could have expected to obey his demands: they were the middle-ranking bureaucrats, formed and nurtured by the Communist system, owing their livelihood to the apparat, and the very people who would most welcome the return to the old ways of Communist orthodoxy that the coup seemed to promise. So in his statement Yeltsin tempered his threats with appeals: he appealed to the army not to shoot on the people; he appealed to the people to stage massive protest strikes and demonstrations; and he appealed to foreign heads of state and government to come to his aid, saying the Yanayev regime was determined to return the world to the era of the cold war. Hurried phone calls to George Bush and John Major appealing to them not to recognize the new regime added to the impression that Yeltsin was surrounded and staging a last stand for democracy, just as the Czechoslovak and Hungarian patriots had done decades earlier.

While Yeltsin was stating his position in the Russian parliament, his foes were doing the same on the other side of town. In the conference hall of the Soviet Foreign Ministry, Gennady Yanayev and four of his co-conspirators took to the stage before the world's press: the atmosphere was electric, tenser than any press conference ever held in the building. The vast majority of the journalists present had nothing but contempt for the men who appeared before them – all wanted the answers to a series of vital questions: were the coup leaders preparing to use force to maintain their grip on power? What had they done with Mikhail Gorbachov, and could they refute persistent rumours that the President had been executed? How did they explain their lip-service support of democracy when they had just ridden roughshod over every democratic norm? What were their intentions regarding international politics, and were they about to initiate a new era of East–West confrontation?

At first the men on stage appeared confident, relaxed, even jovial. Yanayev corrected one questioner who referred to him as a member of the politburo, but added genially, 'Those sort of distinctions are not important now.' Next to him, Boris Pugo, the hardline Interior Minister, tried hard to smile, but succeeded only in appearing more wild-eyed and unhinged than ever, his mad-professor hair shooting out around the sides of his bald pate. Absent from the press conference were KGB chief Vladimir Kryuchkov and Defence Minister Dmitri Yazov: it was assumed they had more important things to do, despatching tanks around the country. Also missing was the boorish Prime Minister Valentin Pavlov, nicknamed hedgehog-bum because of his peasant-style crew cut; we learned later that he had been hitting the bottle a little too hard.

With hindsight it is easy to see the eight conspirators as bumbling no-hopers destined to fail, but on that Monday afternoon they were the men who held ultimate power in the Soviet Union, and the questioning from the floor was hostile. Yanayev's first tactic was to suggest the takeover was designed to protect the reforms which been taking place in the country but which had run into the sand. 'At a crucial moment for the Soviet Union and for the whole world,' he said, 'the crisis we have come up against must not be allowed to continue. This would threaten the whole of our reform programme and lead to a serious cataclysm in international life.' But it did not take long for the double talk to be replaced with something more straightforward. Ynayev warned:

> The country is beginning to disintegrate and we are determined to take the most serious measures to prevent this . . . to reimpose law and order, and to clean the criminals from our streets. . . . In international politics, we wish to live in peace, but we state firmly that we will not allow any outside forces to infringe our national sovereignty, independence and territorial integrity. . . . we are not afraid of expressing our pride and patriotism, and we are determined to bring up our coming generations in this same spirit . . . it is the duty of every citizen of the Soviet Union to give support to the State Emergency Committe as it carries out its programme.

After repeated questioning about the fate of Mikhail Gorbachov – who was now widely believed to be a prisoner in the hands of the putschists – Yanayev had the effrontery to urge us cynically not to worry:

> Mikhail Gorbachov is still enjoying rest and recuperation at the Crimean holiday location where he was on vacation when taken ill. He has become very tired after all his years in power and he will need a goodly length of time to recover his health. . . . I even hope that when he has recovered he may one day be able to return to his duties as President. . . . Mikhail Gorbachov did a great deal to initiate democratic processes in our country in 1985, and he deserves all our respect.

Coming from the lips of the man who had just ordered Gorbachov's arrest, such sentiments carried the stamp of a politician with more gall than integrity.

The next line of questioning, however, was enough to remove all traces of Yanayev's previous cockiness. What, he was asked, do you think about Boris Yeltsin's statement this afternoon in which he describes your accession to power as a right-wing, reactionary, anti-constitutional coup? Yeltsin's words – and the implied threat of concerted opposition to the new regime – seemed to throw Yanayev into a panic. His face began to twitch and his fingers twisted nervously on the desk in front of him. 'We of course are ready to cooperate with Mr Yeltsin to develop democracy, the economy, culture and human rights. But. . . .' – and here he paused to swallow hard – 'if Yeltsin is calling for general strikes, then he's acting very irresponsibly and that's something we can't allow. The country is in crisis. . . . the Russian leadership are now playing a very dangerous political game. This could lead to excesses and armed provocations. It is the duty of the State Emergency Committee to warn all Soviet people about this. We trust that calm and order will be maintained in all areas.'

When pressed about the way he had come to power, Yanayev looked grim. 'I will permit myself to disagree with your contention that a state coup has taken place,' he said. 'We are acting according to the norms of the constitution. I can tell you that the decision we took will be approved by the Supreme Soviet when it meets and this will prove that absolutely all legal and constitutional processes have been observed. To compare our actions to a coup is incorrect, and I say that to do so is simply very dangerous.'

Like all new dictators, though, Yanayev had a carrot as well as a stick. Taking his cue from Augusto Pinochet, who consolidated his coup d'etat in Chile by bringing about enough economic prosperity to distract the people's attention from the illegality of his takeover, Yanayev began promising the earth: there would be more flats and more food, he said; prices would be frozen or drastically cut, while wages would be doubled. The competent organs had been instructed to take measures 'within a week' to slash prices for consumer goods and food, children's items and communal services (transport, gas, electricity etc.), while it would take 'two weeks' to increase all wages, pensions, grants and subsidies.

They were, of course, promises from Wonderland with no chance of being fulfilled, and in the end they never had to be put to the test. But my impression was that it was this sort of rhetoric, together with promises to stamp out crime and restore the rule of law, which won the coup leaders a sizeable amount of support from parts of the population. In the first days of the coup, signs of popular backing for the putsch were not hard to find – a split in public sentiment which made it hard to predict with any certainty that the coup would fail. After all, similar tactics in October 1964 had contributed to the downfall of Nikita Khrushchev: in the days before his removal, hardline sabotage meant that food virtually disappeared from the shops, allowing Khrushchev's opponents to discredit him and to take the popular credit for re-stocking the shelves once they had seized power.

But Yanayev could not resist ending his press conference with a spectacular return to the big stick. The State Emergency Committee, he said, had decided to extend the temporary extraordinary measures in Moscow by carving the city into a series of thirty-three military districts each with a military commandant to ensure the Committee's orders were executed. In overall charge of the city would be Colonel-General Nikolai Kalinin and his deputy Lieutenant-General Nikolai Myrikov, who would between them exercise emergency powers to maintain order – virtually a carte blanche for the military to use any means they deemed necessary to fulfil the political goals of the new regime. At their disposal would be troops of the Moscow garrison, the Soviet Interior Ministry, the Moscow Interior Ministry, the Moscow KGB and the Moscow Region KGB.

The troops would be empowered to take over any factory or enterprise which looked like going on strike, to run all public transport in the capital and to control most aspects of public life. Demonstrations, rallies, meetings, street processions and strikes had, of course, already been banned; now, even sports events, public entertainment including theatres and cinemas, and other seemingly harmless activities would need the permission of the military district commander before being allowed to take place. Political parties or groupings deemed not to support the 'normalization process' being undertaken by the New Kremlin leadership were suspended with immediate effect. The army would be encouraged to search apartments, cars and pedestrians (without needing a search warrant) in order to locate and destroy 'firearms and knives, ammunition, explosives, poisons and narcotics, as well as handwritten or printed materials calling for violation of public order'; those found in possession of such materials would be 'brought to account in accordance with the law'.

Most worrying was Yanayev's announcement of tough curfew measures for the city, details of which were published the following day. These consisted of a ban on all movement between the hours of 11 p.m. and 5 a.m. Citizens were 'prohibited from staying outside their apartments, on the streets or in other public places without special passes and identification'. Those found without valid documents would be 'taken to militia headquarters, searched and detained for a period defined by the law'. A round-the-clock ban was imposed on vehicles from outside Moscow trying to enter the city (except for those ensuring the operation of industrial enterprises, catering, trade or children's school activities), and the army was instructed to suppress rigorously 'all instances of spreading of provocative rumours, actions provoking violations of law and order, active resistance to implementation of legal orders as well as wilful non-compliance with instructions from an Interior Ministry official'. Those detained on such charges would face heavy fines or prison sentences.

At the end of Yanayev's news conference, there was little doubt left that the junta was tough, ruthless and determined to crush any opposition to its authority; and even though estimates of the regime's efficiency were revised over the next three days, the first signs were that the repression had already begun.

Arriving back at BBC Television's office in the Belorusskii station district, we found waiting for us the former KGB colonel turned dissident, and now radical member of the Soviet parliament, Oleg Kalugin. Through his remaining contacts within the KGB he had learnt that a campaign of mass arrests was under way. The targets were liberal politicians, activists and potential supporters of the resistance campaign initiated by Boris Yeltsin. Kalugin said he had already had notification of several arrests, including that of Telman Gdlyan, the radical prosecutor who had earlier aroused the fury of the conservatives by fingering old guard leader, Yegor Ligachov, in a corruption probe, and who was now an active figure in the liberal opposition movement. Kalugin said he had also learnt that a warrant had been issued for his own arrest, and he had had to take precautions like switching trains and buses on his way to our office to avoid being detained.

Kalugin's information about the KGB crack-down and those taken into custody was later confirmed to be accurate, so there is little reason to doubt his assertion that more dramatic measures – with a more irreversible outcome than mere arrest – were being prepared for Boris Yeltsin and his colleagues who were still holding out in the Russian parliament building.

Yeltsin's stand at the White House had by now become the focal point for all opposition to the junta. The episode with the tanks outside the parliament earlier in the afternoon had revived ominous memories of the previous attempted putsches in Latvia and, in particular, Lithuania, where President Vytautas Landsbergis had taken refuge in his parliament and called for pro-democracy supporters to defend the building with their lives. In Lithuania, the presence of hundreds of civilians outside the parliament had deterred any frontal assault by the tanks, although similar human cordons did not deter a murderous attack to seize the Vilnius television tower, or – later – a similar massacre of unarmed defenders outside the Latvian Council of Ministers building. So when Yeltsin began to appeal for civilians to gather around the White House – his appeals broadcast on his shoestring short-wave radio station, but circulated much more efficiently by Moscow's astoundingly extensive word-of-mouth grapevine – those who responded knew the real and present danger they were exposing themselves to.

The crowds really began to build up from around dusk. Arriving from work, or from colleges and the university, they came first in dribs and drabs, then in larger numbers and finally in their thousands. The emotion of the occasion was all-embracing. These were ordinary men and women, some mere school boys, others gnarled working men, others elderly pensioners or invalids, many of them women toughened by endless hours spent standing in Soviet queues. They were not special; they were not politicians or heroes; they were the people – the *narod* – finally ready to stand up for their rights. They were the living evidence that reform in the Soviet Union had not been in vain: for all its shortcomings, and even if it was now about to be snuffed out, perestroika had created these men and women who were ready to suffer, to fight and – if necessary – to die in defence of what they knew was right.

Prior to 1985 this could not have happened: people then were so cowed and down-trodden that whatever injustices or crimes were inflicted on them by whatever regime was in power, they would have swallowed hard and accepted it. But now the people had seen that life could be different. They knew it would be a long and difficult road before that new life was attained, a life based on human values, with respect for the individual; but they had started on that road and they were determined not to be pushed off it. And, in the end, that was why the thousands who came to the Russian parliament that evening considered that all the discomfort and risks to their personal safety were worth taking. There was a tacit understanding among those present that the political battle-lines had been drawn during the day, the rhetoric and the statements were over, and that it was now down to the people to fight the physical battle on the streets which would really decide the future of the country.

★   ★   ★

It wasn't the best sort of weather for an all night vigil that Monday evening. There wasn't the bitter cold and snow covered ground of the Baltic vigils in January, but it was damp and dark, a seemingly moonless night on which any sensible person would be sitting at home with the vodka bottle open. At first, there was little organization to the gathering. People wandered aimlessly around outside the vast four-square parliament building with its ramps and stairs and identical entrances on each facade; and the parliament towered above us, its white bulk still managing to glow faintly in the dark, its towering filigree clock turret and flag still reaching vaguely towards the heavens. For the next forty-eight hours the parliament and its grounds would be our constant home, and by the end the building took on an almost mythical character, a white ghost leading us through the darkness, an outward and visible sign of an inward and spiritual concept that we were all defending. In his poem, Yevtushenko addresses the parliament as a 'wounded marble swan of freedom, defending by the people and swimming onwards to immortality'.

At the start it was all rather an adventure. The crowds of half-perceived faces in the dark, sometimes gathering round the scattered bonfires or bursting into sporadic singing, reminded me of the Latvian volunteers at the Riga TV station in January. They had stayed there for weeks on end, hoping to keep the tanks at bay; and the Moscovites who turned out now had no way of knowing how long they too would have to forsake their homes and families to pass their nights in the dank grounds of a marble parliament. But most were cheerful, and those who had too much nervous energy could always lend a hand building the barricades.

It will remain a mystery to me where all the material came from to build those makeshift tank traps and barriers. Everything from park benches, steel water pipes and the contents of entire construction sites pitched up there that evening. At every entrance or approach road to the parliament (and it is a big building: it takes fifteen minutes just to walk round it), some form of barricade had been erected by the early hours of Tuesday morning. In truth, they looked incapable of stopping a concerted tank attack; they were nothing like the welded, semi-permanent cordon we had admired around the Lithuanian parliament, or the vast granite blocks lifted by cranes onto the streets of Riga under siege; but they were good for morale. We felt a little safer with a few concrete slabs piled up between us and the street, and they gave something positive to concentrate on instead of worrying endlessly about what was likely to be coming in our direction.

The barricades, though, did make movement around the parliament more difficult, and it was eventually decided to assign sections of the crowd to individual sectors of the building's perimeter, where they were meant to stay come what may. And that was the start of the home-grown organization which sprang up to keep order among the defenders during the coming hours and days. In each section, stewards (known as the *starshii*, or the elders) were appointed and their writ was law on the territory they were given to control. The stewards slowly managed to assign each defender a particular position in a concentric pattern of human chains around the parliament. Every half hour or so, the stewards would shout 'To your places', and a dress rehearsal of how we were to meet the tanks would take place, with everyone linking arms in chains which were eventually four or five rows deep right round the building.

As usually happens at communal events in Russia, food and drink also started to appear, men and women turning up with half a dozen sausages, some home-made soup or a few loaves of bread, and passing through the crowds handing food out to all who were hungry – a simple act of communion, of giving and taking, which made us all feel part of a common cause. Hard drink, though, was rigorously banned, and anyone who turned up looking the worse for a few tipples was firmly escorted away from the area, the stewards explaining that it had been agreed we must give the junta no reason to criticize our behaviour, to accuse us of provocation, or to find an excuse – however flimsy – for sending in the forces of law and order. (Drunkenness was a favourite explanation for state brutality: it was one of the reasons put forward for the Tbilisi massacre in April 1989, and – although we did not yet know it – it would be used again twenty-four hours after we first gathered at the parliament, when three young Russians were killed by the army.)

As the night wore on, the level of discipline and organization increased. The main entrance of the parliament towers above the Moskva river, where steps descend to the embankment. But it was the back of the building, surrounded by the grounds of a small ornamental park, which was chosen as the nerve centre. From the balcony overlooking the crowds below, large Russian flags were hung (tricolours, pre-revolutionary, without the hammer and sickle of course), and a public address system was set up to broadcast information about political developments, tactics, the movements of tanks in the city and – more prosaically – when the next consignment of bread and cheese was due to arrive. The public address system turned out to be a vital tool: it kept the spirit of communal responsibility going, and it helped defuse the circulation of rumours and scare stories (although Yeltsin's lieutenants later showed they were not averse to using it to put out their own false information when they felt it might help to boost sagging morale among their defenders).

In the early hours of Tuesday morning, though, the announcement which drew the greatest applause was not about food. It was the news we had all been hoping for, but had barely dared to expect: part of the Soviet army had agreed to defect and was coming to help us defend the parliament. After seemingly endless reports of tanks moving into yet another area of the city, it was the first encouraging sign that a split in the military – crucial to any hopes for a successful defence, and even an eventual defeat of the hardline army commanders – might after all be about to happen. What was more, the troops we were told to expect were from the elite Taman Guards, the pride and joy of the military establishment and the regiment the authorities trotted out when they wanted to impress foreign visitors with the discipline, efficiency and loyalty of the Soviet defence forces.

Later announcements on the public address system spoke of further defections in the Kantemirovskii regiment outside Moscow and among the crack paratroopers based in Ryazan. We were told to expect their arrival imminently, and – wonder of wonders – a tank detachment which had also decided to join our cause. Much repeated and slightly apprehensive warnings over the tannoy system stressed to the crowds that these would be friendly tanks, that our defences should be lifted to make way for them to come through, and that no mistakes should be made about attacking them in error.

When the armour did arrive – a dozen or so light field tanks – the crews were greeted as heroes. An overwhelming feeling of relief, that we were not alone against the world after all, swept through the crowd, and there were a few tears in the eyes of even the most grizzled faces. The barricades were swiftly opened – it only took a few minutes to roll way the iron pipes and packing cases – and the tanks were posted at strategic points around the building. The main concentration of fire-power was located at the corner of the parliament which looks towards Kutuzovsky Prospekt, because that is where any frontal assault was thought most likely to come from. (Early the next morning, buses and tramcars were positioned to block Kutuzovsky where it passes over the bridge in front of the Ukraine Hotel: the intention was to slow down or stop the advancing Soviet forces long enough to give our friendly tanks a chance to loose off a few heavy rounds at them in the hope of preventing a close quarters battle at the parliament itself.) Some of our other tanks were taken round behind the parliament to protect the nerve centre at the back of the building, although an assault was considered less likely from this direction as the approaching streets were narrow and more easily blocked.

It was here, too, that the ominous sight of mobile field hospitals began to appear. They were manned by volunteers from local clinics and surgeries and I was told they had the capacity to treat up to three hundred casualties at a given time. Looking at the meagre supplies of plasma and bandages, though, I suspected this was a vast overestimate, or that a casualty would receive very perfunctory treatment. When the rain began to pour down before dawn on Tuesday, the area of grass on which the hospital was laid out was quickly trampled into a sea of mud, and I made a mental note that if I were to be wounded I would do my utmost to avoid letting them treat me there!

Throughout the night there were sporadic alarms among the crowds: the public address system would periodically call for a general alert, and it was never clear whether it was yet another drill or the real thing this time. But as day broke the consensus seemed to be that the chances of an attack were now less likely. It was a time to stretch tired limbs after standing all night or lying on the soaked grass; and for some it was time to go back to the jobs they had left the previous evening to come here. The crowds began to thin out as morning came, and those of us with cars were called on to help ferry out the elderly or infirm. I took one woman back into town who must have been at least seventy. When I expressed admiration for her dedication in taking part in the blockade, she gave the explanation that was to be repeated so many times over the next two days (especially by Russian women, for whom Boris Yeltsin has a specially deep attraction): 'Well you see, deary,' she said, 'we have to protect our Borya, don't we? He's the only hope we've got left. And anyway,' she added, 'it's not me you should feel sorry for, but my son here: he's broken his back twice in the last year, he's registered as a ninety per cent invalid, and yet he spent the whole night on his feet, and he's going to do it again tomorrow. . . .'

2

Tuesday, 20 August

The drama of Monday had left us alarmed, but relieved that a full-scale assault had not materialized. There were those who said we were foolish to reduce the numbers around the parliament, because day-time was no guarantee that the army would not attack. Experience in the Baltics, though, suggested that the military did prefer night-time to do its dirty business, so the daylight hours of Tuesday were widely considered to be a moment of reprieve, an opportunity to strengthen defences and prepare for the battle which everyone now expected once the sun went down.

But before that could happen, the people of Moscow had a final chance to show what they thought of the Yanayev regime, to demonstrate to the men in the Kremlin, and to the world, that if they were doomed once again to be subjugated to an oppressive Communist junta, they would not go meekly. In response to calls from Boris Yeltsin and radicals in the Russian parliament, and from the liberal Moscow City Council (Mossoviet), the people were to turn out on Manezhnaya Square at eleven in the morning. The declared aim of the rally's organizers was a peaceful demonstration under the walls of the Kremlin to demand the reinstatement of Mikhail Gorbachov. But Moscow's rumour mill was working overtime that morning, and the talk of the city was that there would be some attempt to enter the Kremlin, possibly to bring about the forceful ejection of the usurpers of power.

In such an atmosphere, and with all demonstrations officially banned since the previous day, there was a mood of trepidation as the time for the rally drew near. It appeared certain that the army would not allow its authority to be flaunted in the centre of Moscow; it was equally certain that the thousands of would-be demonstrators were not going to flinch from a clash, and the prospect of bloodshed seemed to come a step nearer.

In front of the Bolshoi Theatre, next to Manezh, we found units of riot troops drawn up the full length of Neglinnaya Street – more than I had ever encountered for a city centre demonstration in the past. The mood was different too. During the Gorbachov years, with a few exceptions, the troops deployed to control demonstrations adopted a low-profile approach, not seeking confrontation and usually prepared for a certain amount of good-natured banter with the crowd. But when we tried to speak to the men deployed at the Bolshoi, we were met with curses and threats from narrow-eyed Central Asians. Marshal Yazov was clearly not prepared to risk using Slav troops to combat a largely Slav demonstration, and the importation of units from the far corners of the Union was, it seemed, another signal that he was serious about the use of force. Later, when we tried to film a unit deployed on Gorky Street, their commander gave the order to rough us up – something which riot troops in previous times had been reluctant to do (presumably under orders from Gorbachov not to offend the foreign press and, through them, foreign public opinion).

The biggest surprise, though, was still to come. As we turned the corner into Manezhnaya Square, we were faced with an astounding sight. From the Lenin Museum, past the Moskva Hotel and across the vast square as far as the Nationalnaya Hotel, an unbroken line of tanks had been formed, with their crews standing in front of them cradling automatic weapons. In the background the Kremlin towers were visible, and behind those towers were the men who had ordered this extraordinary show of strength. Further inquiries revealed that every approach to the Kremlin had ben sealed off in a similar manner, making certain that no crowds could come within three hundred yards. For a regime which claimed to have the confidence of the people, the new men in power were making very serious efforts to keep that people at bay. It was, in effect, a return to the Stalinist ethic of complete separation between rulers and ruled, an approach which had been progressively broken down by the more open style of government adopted under Gorbachov.

Grim soldiers stared impassively as Yeltsin's supporters arrived in the square, having already run the gauntlet of closed roads and saturation policing of an area that stretched from one to two miles on all sides of the Kremlin. Even the most stubborn of the rally's organizers realized that there was no prospect of breaching such a cordon of steel, and stewards with megaphones were deployed to redirect demonstrators up the hill onto Gorky Street. The crowds thus began to move away from the Kremlin and towards the Moscow City Council building, where a large open square opposite had been designated as an alternative site. This change of direction involved opening a line of tanks which had been deployed across Gorky Street to stop crowds approaching the Kremlin from the other direction. The unit's commander was reluctant to do so (lack of orders seemingly outweighing the presence of common sense), but was eventually prevailed on to comply when it became clear that the crowd had no other way to leave if he did not step back.

Several thousand people eventually gathered in the square under a constant drizzle, carrying banners condemning the coup and chanting 'Yanayev – Judas, Fascism – out'. They heard speeches from the balcony of the City Council building. Eduard Shevardnadze and Aleksandr Yakovlev – the two men who had warned in advance that a military putsch was being planned – drew the greatest applause for their support of Yeltsin's stand, and for their demands that the coup leaders be removed and brought to trial. Shevardnadze repeated his gloomy assessment that the new regime was on the point of destroying all the foreign policy successes of the Gorbachov years and plunging the whole world back into cold war. But the speech which struck me in particular came from Sergei Stankevich, the young, articulate and clean-cut former Deputy Mayor of Moscow who had just been appointed a Senior Counsellor in the leadership of Boris Yeltsin's Russian Federation.

Stankevich started by asking the crowd what they thought of the coup – were they angry about it? did they regret it had taken place? 'Well,' said Stankevich, 'I am glad the coup happened'. Silence from the crowd. 'I'm glad,' he said, 'because now we know who is who. We've seen who those bastards are who want to overthrow democracy: this putsch has flushed them all out into the open; and when we get back to power, we're going to have them all put away.' The tumultuous applause was natural. Stankevich's certainty that things would turn out for the best was probably intended only to boost morale; but it was one of a number of statements which were later cited by journalists seeking to suggest that the whole coup had been stage-managed by the liberals and by Gorbachov – or at least carried out with their tacit blessing – to rid them of their hardline enemies in one fell swoop.

At the time, though, the crowd was less concerned with conspiracy theories than with the reaction of the troops sent by the conspirators in the Kremlin. Perhaps because of the weather, perhaps because of a fear of clashes with the army or because of army harassment on the way, or perhaps because a substantial percentage of the population secretly supported the coup and did not want to speak against it, the turn-out at the rally had been disappointingly small: several thousand, instead of the hundreds of thousands who had come to similar pro-Yeltsin demonstrations in peacetime. As a result, there was never any real threat of a storming of the Kremlin and the security forces presumably decided not to risk unnecessary bloodshed, eventually allowing the meeting to go ahead unhindered.

But in the eyes of many present, the lack of army intervention was another psychological victory for the democrats: the crowds had defied the Kremlin simply by demonstrating and had got away with it. The regime was made to look weak because it had banned demonstrations but then had not had the courage or the consistency to enforce its own decree. It was the second example of disarray by the junta (the first was over the Yeltsin speech on the back of the tank outside the Russian parliament), and it was not to be the last.

Buoyed by their success, the demonstrators unfurled a massive tricoloured Russian flag – almost one hundred yards long – as a symbol of their support for Yeltsin and his Russian democrats. The flag was then carried triumphantly on the heads of the crowd as they marched up Gorky Street, onto the inner ring-road and down to the Russian parliament itself. They arrived to a joyous reception from the defenders who had remained in place there during the morning, the flag being lifted onto the balcony at the rear of the parliament and fixed in place to mark the organizational centre of the operation to defend the building.

As stragglers and new arrivals from other parts of the city began to roll in, the numbers outside the parliament reached a high point of about fifty thousand – at last, the display of solidarity that the Yeltsin campaign so desperately needed. Their almost continuous chants of 'Yeltsin, Yeltsin!' must eventually have reached the ears of the man who had now been inside the parliament for more than twenty-four hours, and to storms of applause Boris himself emerged onto the balcony.

The speech that Yeltsin made that Tuesday afternoon was a rhetorical masterpiece, restoring the flagging morale of those who had been at the parliament since the previous day, on their feet virtually the whole time, with no sleep and little rest, and who were, not surprisingly, beginning to wonder whether they would ever see their homes again. At his bombastic best, Yeltsin began his address with a gloomy assessment of what would happen if the plotters were allowed to get away with their seizure of power. 'The shadows of darkness,' he said, to apprehensive silence from the crowd, 'have descended on our country, on Europe and on the world.' The apprehension of the defenders was aroused; the enormous import of their task made crystal clear. And then Yeltsin went on to raise our spirits, our pride and our belief that we could ultimately triumph. 'I have resolved,' he said, 'to resist these men, these usurpers in the Kremlin.' (He used the word *samozvantsy*, redolent with historical overtones of imposters or pretenders who had dared to seize the God-given power of legitimate rulers and who suffered the bloody consequences of their temerity.) 'I have resolved this, and I call on you to do the same!' (Applause and cries of 'We are with you, Boris!'.) 'Without your help, I can do nothing' (murmurs from the crowd) '. . . but together with you, and with the Russian people, we are capable of the greatest feats of heroism: we are capable of defeating these putschists and ensuring the triumph of democracy!'

The emotional catharsis of the moment was completed by a deafening roar of approval from the crowd. From being a disoriented and slightly uncertain mob, those present were transformed into dedicated, fearless enthusiasts, determined now to stay at their posts, full of personal loyalty to Boris Yeltsin and fired with the belief that they could change the course of history.

On the parliament's balcony, Yeltsin was flanked by men who had proved their commitment to the cause of democracy and who were about to prove the courage of their convictions by remaining with him throughout the denouement of the coup. They were Eduard Shevardnadze and Aleksandr Yakovlev; Stanislav Shatalin, the elderly and frail economist; Gavriil Popov, the radical mayor of Moscow; Sergei Stankevich; and Yeltsin's team of close advisers led by his Vice-President Aleksandr Rutskoi. These and others who rallied to the Russian parliament secured their reputations and their political future: presence on the barricades later became a litmus test of who could be trusted and who could not, in the same way that those who took part in, supported or did not oppose the coup were to become political pariahs. Only Mikhail Gorbachov, who was off the scene during the crucial hours of the coup, was to be left in an ambiguous position. Apart from the mysteries surrounding his role, the coup was to polarize Soviet politics with seemingly irreversible effect.

The role of the Soviet people was also under scrutiny that afternoon: those who came to the parliament or demonstrated on the streets had made their own decisive choice in favour of democracy. But there were, in truth, not that many of them: fifty thousand people from a city of ten million is not an overwhelming percentage. Many more may have opposed the coup in their hearts, but they did little or nothing to put that emotion to practical effect. Strikes did occur sporadically, but most enterprises kept going and there were enough transport workers willing to work to keep the buses and the metro in action. At this stage of the coup, Yeltsin was facing not only the Kremlin's tanks, but also the apathy of large sections of the population.

Even more challenging was the sentiment expressed by a considerable number of ordinary Soviets that the coup leaders should be given a chance, that they could hardly do worse than the previous lot in power, and that they might at least bring back law and order. Especially attractive to many people were the plotters' promises of ending the rise in crime, the spiralling ethnic conflicts which were dogging the country, and the attempts of independence-minded republics to break up the Union. The latter appealed to Soviet patriotism, as did Yanayev's talk of restoring the USSR's position and pride in the eyes of the world; but few who parroted Yanayev's words had thought for how these results would be achieved, for the inevitable bloodshed and suffering which would attend a campaign to repress the demands of ethnic minorities or republics, or for the international tensions which would flow from a reassertion of Moscow's old aggressive image in world politics. There had been serious problems under perestroika: material living conditions had worsened dramatically, discipline had fallen and crime had become a real issue; so it was understandable that some people would look to the junta as Italians did to Mussolini to 'make the trains run on time'. But in the final analysis, most of those who did not oppose the coup were probably, quite simply, scared.

Boris Yeltsin and his allies that Tuesday afternoon might well have hoped to arouse a much wider spectrum of public support. For the parliament's defenders, the laurels of triumph still looked a long way off as dusk began to fall, and with it all the fears of a night which most of us expected to be decisive. Rumours of an imminent storming of the building by Soviet forces had been growing since late afternoon. Announcements over the parliament's public address system had become more breathless, and general alerts among the defenders more frequent.

The tanks which had defected to Yeltsin's cause were still in place around the parliament, but they were lightly armoured vehicles and there were relatively few of them. What had looked and sounded immensely impressive as they roared into our midst in darkness the previous night had turned out in daylight to be a little less imposing. The paratroopers who had come over were – we assumed – inside the building preparing for the sort of hand-to-hand combat which had happened in January at the Vilnius TV tower, but the crowds outside could not see them so drew little comfort from their presence. The forces which had joined Yeltsin were not large, and they did not constitute proof of any major divisions within the army command – certainly not a split of the magnitude which would be needed to make a battle on the streets anything other than a one-sided walkover. Only a few hundred yards away, on the Kutuzovsky bridge over the Moskva river, the Kremlin's own tanks were in position, watching the goings-on at the parliament and ready to strike if ordered to do so. No one doubted that Marshal Yazov had at his command the endless supply of tank reinforcements which we so plainly lacked.

With the odds stacked against him, Yeltsin started to play the propaganda game. After dark on Tuesday evening his staff invited foreign journalists into the central part of the parliament building to see the inner offices which had been fortified against attack. Yeltsin did not appear, except as a fleeting presence moving between one corridor and another: we were told that he and his closest aides had a special inner sanctum which was the most heavily guarded and could be best defended if the building was stormed. We were not invited to visit Yeltsin's bunker, but the internal defences we were allowed to see were not impressive. In some offices sand bags had been piled against doors and windows, but in most cases it was simply a question of stacking filing cabinets and tables in the way of an onrushing enemy.

The paratroopers were there, though, and they looked confident and well prepared. They had spread their sleeping rolls on the floor of one of the committee rooms and – unlike us – they were not too nervous to get some rest, their weapons laid beside them on the floor ready for an urgent call to action. Several well-known deputies from the Russian and Soviet legislatures were also present, some of them carrying machine guns. Most of them looked as though they would probably have difficulty making the things work, and might well turn out to be a bigger danger to their own side than to the enemy. But it was clearly important for them to be there, and carrying a gun was the most potent symbol of their dedication and readiness for self-sacrifice that they could create.

Also carrying a gun, but looking rather more professional about it, was the Russian Vice-President Aleksandr Rutskoi. An intriguing character, Rutskoi was a former Soviet air force lieutenant; he had served longer in Afghanistan than nearly any other officer, been twice captured by the Mujehadin rebels and – according to all reports – horrifically tortured before escaping. When the war was over, he came back to Moscow and went into political life, first as a hardline Communist, spouting all the orthodox slogans but campaigning for servicemen's rights. His disillusionment at the system's failure to look after former soldiers was said to have prompted a radical rethinking of his political values and he swerved to the radical wing of the Communist party, eventually participating in a liberal 'Communists for Democracy' faction which supported Yeltsin in parliament. Rutskoi's reward was the offer to run with Yeltsin on the winning ticket for the Russian presidency, and his presence in the besieged parliament was now proving remarkably useful. With his personal hand-gun slung in its leather holster across his chest, Rutskoi explained in a matter-of-fact way that he was not intending to surrender if the troops came in to get him. 'I know the sort of bastards we're up against,' he said, 'and I know we have to fight to the end.'

Other members of Yeltsin's staff told us they knew of plans by the KGB and Special Forces to storm into the building and shoot out every person on the first and second floors. They said they knew that orders had been given for Yeltsin and his closest aides to be shot, with the troops specifically instructed not to take any prisoners. This was the story which Yeltsin himself was to repeat after the coup was over, and it was difficult even at that stage to determine whether he was speaking the truth or merely dramatizing the predicament he found himself in, to stress the inhumanity of his opponents and the bravery of his allies. But on that dark Tuesday night, inside a besieged parliament where all lights had been extinguished in a total black-out for security purposes, the atmosphere was tense enough for the suggestions of a ruthless enemy waiting to burst in firing to unnerve all of us present.

Yeltsin's aides seemed uncertain about what response would be offered in the event of an all out attack. Some suggested Yeltsin himself would attempt to escape via a helicopter from a friendly air force unit, which would land on the roof of the building. Others said there were plans for an evacuation through tunnels under the building.

There was confusion, too, about how the unarmed civilian defenders outside the parliament were meant to react in the event of an assault. The uncompromising Rutskoi seemed to be in favour of all out resistance to keep the tanks at bay, and messages to that effect were initially broadcast to the crowd. But later in the night, when an attack was looking almost certain, Yeltsin finally adopted a radically different approach. In repeated announcements over the public tannoy, it was stressed that civilians should offer no resistance to the army and should step back to let them through. This was, we were informed, on instructions from the President himself.

It is hard to say whether these divergences were the result of disagreements among the Russian leadership, or whether the uncertainty was deliberately sown to leave the army uncertain of the reception it was likely to face. But from the crowd's point of view it was confusing, and even at three o'clock in the morning, when the announcements were consistently advocating no resistance, many of those around me were still determined to fight the tanks come what may.

Inside the parliament that night, though, there was one voice of calm which did much to keep the situation under control. That was the voice of Colonel-General Konstantin Kobets, the Chairman of the Defence and Security Committee of the Russian Council of Ministers. He was the man Yeltsin appointed to oversee the defence of the parliament, and who must take most of the credit for the efficiency of the operation. Kobets directed the construction of the two rings of barricades around the parliament, advising on how best to thwart advancing tanks; and he was the central figure in organizing the thousands of civilian volunteers into a disciplined and responsive defence force. But most of all, Kobets personally directed the collection of intelligence about the movements of Soviet army units in the city, allowing at least some early warning of a potential attack. It was he who tried to negotiate with army commanders in the enemy camp, and who sent envoys to try to persuade Red

Army units to defect: it was thus due to Kobets's activities that the elements of the Taman Guards, the Kantemirovskii Regiment and the Ryazan paratroopers under Colonel-General Grachov came to the parliament's defence.

A year earlier Kobets had been sacked from his post in the Soviet army command when he took a job on Yeltsin's staff, but at the height of the coup during the Tuesday night, Yeltsin was reported to have told Kobets, 'You know, I never trusted you until today'; and, in recognition of his loyalty, Yeltsin promoted him on the spot to the post of Russian Defence Minister.

Events were now moving rapidly towards what looked like being an unpleasant and dangerous battle for the parliament. On Tuesday evening Yeltsin's Foreign Ministry called diplomats from all Western embassies in Moscow to tell them the Russian leadership had firm information that the parliament was about to be stormed, and that they expected this to have bloody consequences. Personal telephone calls from Yeltsin to George Bush and other Western leaders carried the same message, with – it must be assumed – an appeal for the West to intervene with the Yanayev regime to try to avert the carnage.

While the diplomatic activity was continuing, though, the regime had ordered its military forces to stage an unprecedented show of strength on the streets of Moscow. Columns of tanks which had previously been held in reserve in the suburbs were called in to take part in a concerted operation to remove the makeshift road-blocks erected by demonstrators on all the approaches to the Russian parliament. These consisted of buses and lorries, either parked with their wheels removed, or overturned, on roads in concentric circles around the parliament, some of them up to a mile or so away from the building. In many locations the tanks were able to push aside the barricades with little difficulty, but some were not easily removed and clashes with demonstrators took place several times during the night. The most serious was outside the American Embassy on the city's inner ring road.

The reasons behind what happened on the Garden Ring between midnight and 6 a.m. are open to dispute, but the facts are clear and deeply disturbing. At around midnight light army tanks moved in to clear barricades on the ironically named Uprising Square (Ploschad' Vosstaniya) to the right of the US Embassy. These were light barriers and easily pushed aside, but the tank crews for some reason began firing off streams of bullets into the air.

This attracted several hundred demonstrators who had been manning heavier barricades on the far side of the Embassy. When they realized the ammunition being fired was live, the demonstrators ran away from the tanks, past the Embassy and into an underpass on the Garden Ring where it goes under Kalinin Prospekt, about five hundred yards up the hill from the Russian parliament.

Eight armoured personnel carriers followed the demonstrators down the slip road, where the APCs were set upon by crowds leaning over the underpass from the parapets on its side and the bridge above it. Two demonstrators managed to throw a large tarpaulin over the turret of the third APC in the column (number 536), and its crew – unable to see where they were going – panicked, revved up to full speed and ran into the side of the tunnel. The crowd who were in the tunnel ran for cover as the APC reversed and careered towards them, but thirty-seven-year old Volodya Usov was just too slow. He was caught in the tank tracks and crushed, his body dragged along by the APC for about twenty yards. There was later some debate about whether the vehicle's commander had run into the demonstrators while blinded by the tarpaulin, or whether it was a deliberate attempt to scatter the crowd. There was no doubt, though, that the troops on board the APCs fired live rounds into the air at this point, and one demonstrator who tried to pull Volodya Usov's body from under the tank tracks was hit and wounded.

The panic among the troops increased when it became clear that they were now trapped in the tunnel. Some of the APCs had already cleared the underpass, but those behind the crippled number 536 found their exit had been cut off by a line of buses. Their attempts to reverse out of the tunnel were also blocked, by a row of street-cleaning vehicles hastily put in place behind them. As the trapped APCs began rushing backwards and forwards, several demonstrators ran up with pieces of wood or metal spars, trying to thrust them into the tank tracks and disable them. Then the crowd began to attack, using Molotov cocktails which they had fetched from a nearby car, first throwing the home-made bombs from the parapet above, but then surrounding the APCs and pouring petrol over the lead vehicle as it tried to ram the buses blocking its way. This APC was set on fire with the crew still trapped inside (they were later rescued, and the threat of exploding ammunition averted thanks to water brought by the demonstrators themselves to extinguish the blaze).

By now the army's patience had been exhausted and firing broke out from all the trapped vehicles. A bullet fired by one of the soldiers ricocheted off the wall of the tunnel and flew into the crowd on the parapet above. Ilya Krichevsky, a twenty-six year old student who had taken no direct part in the attack on the armoured column, was hit and fatally wounded.

With the APCs repeatedly ramming the line of trolley-buses but unable to break through, the demonstrators were again emboldened to move closer, and that is when the third death occurred. Twenty-three-year-old Dmitri Komar was reported to have been trying to rescue a woman from the path of one of the charging vehicles when he slipped and was drawn under its tracks. He was crushed to death, but a companion who also fell under the APC emerged unscathed, having passed between the tank tracks.

With three demonstrators dead and one vehicle in flames, the army commanders gave the order to switch off the vehicles' engines, batten down the hatches and await help. The stand-off lasted for about half an hour, until the arrival of a delegation from the Moscow District Military command. Led by Lieutenant-General Nikolai Smirnov, the delegation managed to reach a compromise with the crowd to win the APCs' release: the terrified soldiers inside the vehicles would be guaranteed safe passage (the demonstrators had earlier been threatening to lynch them), in return for agreeing to hoist the colours of the Russian republic and renounce their allegiance to the Yanayev regime. The major who had been commanding the APCs reportedly ran away, presumably fearing retribution, but the soldiers themselves agreed to the deal and at six o'clock in the morning the remaining vehicles were driven away in triumph by the demonstrators.

Back at the Russian parliament, the sound of gunfire and revving engines from the incident outside the US Embassy had been clearly audible, and rumours of escalating military action were threatening to spark panic among the crowds of defenders. The public address system periodically broadcast news of tank movements heading in the direction of the parliament, and calls for a general alert were made on three separate occasions, quoting intelligence gathered by the parliamentary defence committee that an attack was imminent. Around two o'clock in the morning it was announced that units of the feared and hated OMON – the special Interior Ministry troops which had carried out the massacres in Latvia and Lithuania – had taken over the former Comecon building on the other side of the street (the building had been unoccupied since Comecon itself collapsed several months earlier), and were preparing to fire on the parliament's defenders. Whether or not this information was true, the threat of death from a sniper's bullet then seemed very real, and it is testimony to the defenders' courage that more of them did not leave at that stage.

Within an hour, the news that three young demonstrators had been killed outside the American Embassy was relayed to the crowd, and everyone present was convinced that we were to be the army's next target. The loudspeakers announced that all women should leave the area. The rest of us who remained behind prepared to meet the tanks. It was the darkest hour of the night, the coup looked about to succeed and democracy in the Soviet Union was all but extinguished.

PART 2

Why Did it Happen?

3

The Spark That Lit
the Fire

With hindsight, the underlying causes of the August coup can be traced back to political currents which had been developing over the whole six years or more of the perestroika period (some of these will be discussed in the following chapters). But at the height of the putsch, when Yanayev's men seemed to have triumphed and the Soviet Union looked destined to return to the control of hardline Marxist-Leninists, anyone with the time to speculate about the immediate reasons for the takeover would only have had to look at the calendar.

On Tuesday 20 August, Mikhail Gorbachov and Boris Yeltsin had not foreseen themselves as prisoners in the Crimea or in the Russian parliament: they had expected to be sitting together in Moscow with the presidents of several of the Soviet republics, signing an historic treaty which would redefine the distribution of power between the centre and those republics willing to be part of a new, revamped USSR. The Union Treaty due to be signed that day was the result of a long process of negotiations, begun initially in response to demands from the Baltic states, Georgia and Moldavia, to leave the Union. Moves towards greater autonomy by Boris Yeltsin's Russia, the largest and most powerful of the fifteen republics, and the ethnic quarrels which had broken out with ferocious violence during the Gorbachov era, had made changes in the power balance necessary and unavoidable.

The simplistic reasoning of Yanayev, Pugo and the others was that this treaty signalled the destruction of the Soviet Union they knew and loved. It ceded to the republics too many of the powers traditionally exercised by the centre (in other words, by the leadership of the Communist Party of the Soviet Union), and – horror of horrors – it accepted the right, albeit with many restrictions, of independence-minded republics to go their own way. In light of the accelerated process of disintegration which took hold after the coup (ironically as a direct result of the plotters' attempts to halt the dismemberment of the empire), the Union Treaty proposed by Gorbachov and accepted in principle by nine of the fifteen republican capitals was remarkable for its restraint and conservatism: the USSR would survive in an altered form, with republics still allowing the centre to exercise certain powers, and measures would be taken to preserve economic links not only between those who accepted the treaty but even among the regions which opted out of the Union.

The plotters showed no signs of accepting the need for any changes in the country's political structure. All they saw was the symbol of Gorbachov's treachery in giving in to the demands of the nationalists and liberals who were bent on destroying the motherland. Indeed, the only explicit policy enunciated by Yanayev during the coup had little to do with the values of Marxism-Leninism; it was, instead, a classic formulation of the Russian imperialist ideal, a deeply felt conviction that the boundaries of the Soviet Union are sacred and inviolable, that the whole of the territory accumulated by Russian expansionism over the centuries had become an inalienable part of the country's heritage and that anyone who agreed to dilute that territorial integrity was a traitor to his country.

But in taking their ultimate decision to rescue the motherland, the plotters showed a fateful ignorance of the historical trends which had made a new Union Treaty so vital. Mikhail Gorbachov too had initially started from the viewpoint that the Union must be held together at all costs, but he had eventually accepted that compromise was the only solution. Beginning from January 1990, when he visited Lithuania to assess the strength of separatist feeling, Gorbachov had slowly softened his Unionist stance, first staging a slanted national referendum designed to win an overall majority for keeping the Union together, but then accepting a constitutional mechanism which would allow republics to secede after a five year period of arduous legal wrangling.

In the end, it could be argued that it was Gorbachov's reluctance to accept change, rather than his enthusiasm for it, which proved his downfall. Had he been quicker to make early concessions to the republics, he might have persuaded them to accept a much less radical reform treaty. In late 1988 the Baltics had shown some indications that they would be willing to settle for economic independence alone, while remaining within the Soviet political structure. That was a solution which Gorbachov was eventually to propose a year later, but by then it was too late. His prevarication had let the opportunity slip by, and the republics had already upped their demands. Gorbachov's own ingrained conservatism meant he missed several chances to satisfy the nationalists with what would later have been regarded as rather moderate concessions.

In the spring of 1991, though, Gorbachov did at last seem to accept the need for quick compromises if he were to salvage any sort of unity for his country. He was under growing pressure from the separatists, and Boris Yeltsin's irresistible rise to power had culminated in a landslide victory in elections for the presidency of the Russian republic. The historical pendulum was swinging in the direction of devolution of power away from the centre, and Gorbachov was enough of a realist to recognize this. By the summer he was ready to meet Yeltsin and the other republican leaders at Novo-Ogaryova outside Moscow to initial a draft treaty that went along with nearly all Yeltsin's demands. The centre was to cede economic and political power to the republics, indicating an unprecedented willingness to give ground even on the key issue of the control of revenues: such a concession would give the republics the sole right to impose taxation on their populations, sending on to Moscow only the proportion of their income which they agreed to hand over. In return, the Kremlin would retain control of foreign policy, national defence, communications and security. It was a dramatic reduction in the traditional powers of the centre, but it did maintain Moscow's role as overall arbiter in certain key areas, and under the circumstances that was the best Gorbachov could hope for. He welcomed the draft accord as a workable balance between his authority and the interests of republican presidents like Boris Yeltsin. He even expressed the hope that the six hardline republics, which had been demanding nothing less than full independence, might eventually be tempted by the generous terms of the accord to rethink their positions and accept some agreement of association.

In the eyes of men like Gennady Yanayev and Anatoly Lukyanov, though, the Union Treaty was not so much a reasonable compromise as an unprincipled sell-out. In an article in *Pravda* on the Tuesday when the coup was at its height, Lukyanov spelt out his opposition to an accord which he accused of distorting the wishes of the people. The treaty, he said, betrayed the Supreme Soviet's demand for a unitary economic and financial system, for the strengthening of the concept of state property (in other words, the centre must retain control of natural resources which the treaty was proposing to cede to the republics), and for central control over taxation. What was more, wrote Lukyanov, it did not put an end to the challenge from those republics which were insisting their own laws take precedence over laws laid down by Moscow; and it did not answer 'the demands of the Soviet people for the preservation of the Soviet Union . . . and for its restoration to the status of a great power, capable of exerting a major influence on the international scene'. The treaty, concluded Lukyanov, should be shelved and new measures worked out to keep the Union together.

So the hardliners, it seems, seized power with one immediate aim in mind: to prevent the signing of Gorbachov's Union Treaty and the handing over of power to the nationalists and the liberals. Their actions could be seen, ironically, as the ultimate vindication of Gorbachov's foot-dragging on the road to reform of the Soviet political structure: he had always argued that he could not give away too much too quickly to the republics because of the hardline threat always at his back. In previous times, we had regarded this argument as little more than an excuse by Gorbachov, a fig leaf to cover his own conservative reluctance to concede radical reforms. The coup proved that he had been right, but by then it was too late: Gorbachov had stepped over the line of what the hardliners considered acceptable and they had acted to remove him. It was the ultimate tragedy of a man who had long been caught between two political extremes, who had sought to please them both and had ended by pleasing neither. As the following chapter will suggest, Gorbachov's conflict with the conservatives did not mean he was any more appreciated by the liberals: it was just that the hardliners had more dramatic ways to show their displeasure.

The conservatives, in fact, had made little attempt to hide their wrath over the Union Treaty, and Gorbachov could in no sense argue that he had not been forewarned. (He seems to have been aware of the hardline sentiment against him, but to have underestimated their capacity to act. When Vladimir Kryuchkov called him on the eve of the coup, demanding that he cooperate or face the consequences, Gorbachov is said to have replied, 'You are just a bunch of no-hopers'; and Aleksandr Yakovlev reported a conversation in which Gorbachov dismissed his urgent warnings, saying: 'They are cowards; they wouldn't dare. . . .') On 22 July an open letter had been published in the hardline newspaper *Sovietskaya Rossiya*, long considered the platform of orthodox Communism in Russia. Entitled 'An appeal to the Russian people', the letter was signed by top military leaders including Colonel Boris Gromov, the Deputy Interior Minister, and General Valentin Varennikov, one of the military's top policy-making commanders, as well as active Slavophile writers like Yuri Bondarev, Aleksandr Prokhanov and Valentin Rasputin. In an unambiguous incitement to revolt, their manifesto asked rhetorically, 'How could we have allowed people to come to power in this country who do not love our fatherland, people who behave like lackeys before their so-called friends from overseas?' It was a clear reference to Gorbachov, who was then in the process of formulating an appeal for aid to the Western industrialized nations of the Group of Seven; and it went on to say that more patriotic leaders could be found in Russia, that the armed forces would support them if they came forward and that it was their sacred obligation to do so.

Already in June a half-hearted attempt to unseat Gorbachov had ended in failure, but even then no lessons seem to have been learned from the experience. Several of the men who eventually led the August coup were involved in the June fiasco: Prime Minister Valentin Pavlov, Interior Minister Boris Pugo, KGB Chief Vladimir Kryuchkov and Defence Minister Dmitri Yazov had all stood up in parliament and demanded that Gorbachov voluntarily renounce his presidential powers. The pretext was that the country's economic problems had become so intense that the government needed a free hand to act unilaterally to solve them. As a consequence, said the motion's proposers, Gorbachov should hand over his right to rule by decree, and his right to declare a state of emergency, to Pavlov. Few believed the rationale advanced by the gang of four: most obervers believed they were intent on a semi-constitutional seizure of power. In the end, the issue never came to a vote in the Supeme Soviet. Hurried negotiations behind the scenes papered over the cracks, and Gorbachov soon returned to the pretence of a united front with his top officials. It was a time of conservative stirrings, and the received wisdom afterwards was that the June revolt was merely another attempt by the hardliners to scare Gorbachov into moving back in their direction after his flirtation with the liberals. Only now is it clear how serious a warning the June episode really was.

But what sort of men were the plotters who tried and failed in June, before trying and failing again with more spectacular consequences in August? Men whom Gorbachov regarded as 'no-hopers' and who had always been seen as *apparatchiks* in the political background? Worms who eventually turned? Deluded patriots?

A couple of weeks before the coup took place, I had been invited to spend an afternoon first with Gennady Yanayev, later to become the titular leader of the junta, and a few days later with Anatoly Lukyanov, the *eminence grise* who masterminded the takeover. Both men were hospitable and seemingly open to any line of questioning, and at the time our interviews took place, both were clearly already involved in planning their coup d'etat.

We were given four separate security checks before reaching Yanayev's office in the heart of the Kremlin, and when we were finally ushered in we were told that the Deputy President was next door 'preparing himself' for our encounter. While we waited, we admired the pre-revolutionary wood panelling and the ornate draperies of the vast, sparsely furnished office. The Kremlin officials who were present told us that the room had been carefully preserved from tsarist times. When I asked about the character of the room's current owner, they shrugged and said, 'His bark is worse than his bite'.

In fact, when Yanayev swept in, he was smiling and full of bonhomie, making an obvious effort to receive us in the grandest of manners.

Small and not particularly well groomed despite his 'preparations', he was demonstratively attentive to the BBC's two women producers, kissing their hands and living up to his reputation as a lady killer by making a not very subtle pass at one of them. In the course of our initial conversation, he made a point of praising my command of Russian. I responded by admiring the splendour of his office, but his only comment was, 'Huh! The parquet floors squeak and they won't let me rip them all out.' He was keen, though, to show us one document which he kept framed on the wall beside his desk. On inspection, this turned out to be the official proclamation signed by Gorbachov appointing him, Gennady Yanayev, to the post of Deputy President.

Everything about Yanayev – his repeated combing of his hair as we were about to start the cameras rolling, the dark glasses to disguise his facial expression, the chain smoking – seemed to speak of a little man thrust into a position of great responsibility. He seemed to enjoy the possession and exercise of power (and later showed himself keen to acquire more of it), but to be slightly overwhelmed by his sudden elevation. He had, after all, been a mere party functionary, making his way through the bureaucracy of the Communist youth movement Komsomol and the official Communist trades unions, until he was plucked from obscurity by Gorbachov at the Congress of Peoples' Deputies on Boxing Day in December 1990.

At that time Gorbachov had spoken highly of Yanayev as a man he could trust, chosen for a position of great importance; he was, said Gorbachov in his speech of recommendation to the Congress, a true devotee of perestroika. Gorbachov's words would later come back to haunt him, and even at that time many members of parliament had doubts about Yanayev. In as much as he was known in the world of politics, he was considered something of a hardline *apparatchik*. He had never questioned the moral value of a trades union movement which was little more than the stooge of the Communist party; and when it came to a vote on his candidature, he was actually rejected by the MPs despite being the only candidate in the race: 583 voted against him, leaving him 34 votes short of the necessary majority. In light of subsequent events, the deputies' first verdict on Yanayev may have been prophetic.

But still Gorbachov persisted, coming to the rostrum with yet another speech of support for his nominee. 'I am sure the only problem is that you do not know Gennady Ivanovich well enough', he told the Congress. 'I am sure that we can come to an agreement. We will agree that the candidacy of Yanayev – when it comes to his personal, political and professional qualities – will be to our liking.' And in a complete travesty of parliamentary procedure, Gorbachov re-submitted Yanayev's name for a second vote. It was, of course, political blackmail by Gorbachov; but on the second time of asking the MPs did his bidding and Yanayev was elected. Gorbachov got the Vice President he wanted, and in doing so he changed the course of history. Yanayev rewarded him for his misguided persistence with an acceptance speech which seemed to justify all the fears of the liberals who had voted against him: 'I am a Communist to the depths of my soul. My principal fight will be against political indiscipline and vandalism', he blustered, adding hastily, '. . . but I will do this through democratic means, not through repression.'

On the afternoon that I sat down to tea with Yanayev in the Kremlin, though, his career as Vice President was still rolling along smoothly. He had not made himself a figure of fun like Dan Quayle in the United States, but neither had he distinguished himself to any great degree. He had stood in for Gorbachov on state occasions, and it was he who had signed the treaty abolishing the Warsaw Pact just a few weeks earlier. But even at that time there were growing rumours that Yanayev had been involved in the June moves against Gorbachov, and I intended to press him on that point. His initial response was simply to deny everything: 'I hope you are not talking about conflicts within the Soviet leadership,' he said. 'The Soviet leadership has a full understanding of the fact that we are all travelling down the same path, and there are no differences between the President, the Vice-President and the Prime Minister.' When I reminded him of the constitutional row in the Supreme Soviet in June, he was dismissive:

> The discussion in the Supreme Soviet is being interpreted as having great political significance. But in fact all that was involved was matters of everyday work. When Prime Minister Pavlov proposed that his Cabinet of Ministers should be given supplementary powers, the issue was not a political revolution or an attempt to undermine the President. No, the issue was that the Cabinet of Ministers needed to have the ability to make speedy decisions on the matters facing us today. So my view is that both the President, and the Supreme Soviet, and the Vice-President, and the Prime Minister and all the key ministers are pulling together as a single team, the team of perestroika, President Gorbachov's team, and there are no grounds for any other interpretation.

Looking back, it seems that the Deputy President did protest a little too much. At one stage he told me, 'I often imagine myself in Mr Gorbachov's position and wonder how I would manage a specific situation.' During the same conversation he almost slipped into talking about Gorbachov in the past tense, saying, 'I think that we should give Mr Gorbachov his due for the courage of the political choice he made in 1985.' He later used the same phrase, almost word for word, at his press conference on 19 August when he celebrated his former boss's overthrow.

Before the coup, the test of a politician's place on the spectrum of liberalism or conservatism was considered to be his attitude towards the importation of Western style, quasi-capitalist economics in the form of a market economy. When I asked him about his views, Yanayev did finally admit that there were splits in the Soviet leadership, and confirmed that he was personally opposed to radical plans for a quick reform of the system. 'If I was to assert that we are all in favour of continuing the policy instituted by President Gorbachov in 1985, I'd be wrong. But there aren't many people with the audacity consciously to impede the transition to a market economy.' Despite repeated protestations of loyalty to perestroika, Yanayev revealed that he was one of the men who did indeed have doubts about a rapid transition to a market economy:

> We have to weigh up the consequences of every step we take. For example, if we adopt the radical Shatalin plan for a market economy,

what would that mean? There are 70 million people in the Soviet Union living on or near the poverty line. If we adopt the Shatalin plan we would have 30 million unemployed by the end of the year. Add it up for yourself: 70 million in or near poverty, plus 30 million unemployed. 100 million makes a powder keg that could destroy our society.

Yanayev was equally dismissive of the leadership's policy of seeking financial aid from the West, a policy championed by Mikhail Gorbachov, which became a favourite target for conservative scorn. 'We are looking for credits – tied credits or unconditional credits. That, I think, is a hopeless policy.' In place of the liberals' policy of cooperation with the West, Yanayev gave the traditional refrain of the conservatives about Soviet pride and self-reliance: 'I think that a people and a country with our traditions, which has survived the most critical periods of history. . . . World War II was not solely a human disaster for us, it also gave us a chance to demonstrate our potential. . . . we survived then, and we'll survive today . . . We are a strong country and we shall deal with our problems.' He was particularly critical of the leadership's acceptance that Western donor countries should be allowed to attach political conditions to their aid: 'Haggling here is entirely inappropriate. The political conditions which some people are trying to impose are not, in my view, a honourable way of approaching this problem.'

In an expression of views which he was later to contradict by his actions during the August coup, Yanayev professed his commitment to political pluralism and a multi-party system. He specifically agreed that the 'imperial ambitions we used to have and which we sometimes tried to realize' now had no future; but he went on to note that 'politics is the art of the possible'. In leading the coup, it later seemed that 'imperial ambitions' were in fact Yanayev's most compelling motivation.

Despite his efforts to present himself as a loyal supporter of perestroika and Gorbachov, Yanayev's innate conservatism showed through several times during our conversations, and in some fascinating final remarks he hinted at the deep-seated fanaticism which was later to push this seemingly innocuous functionary into the greatest political gamble of recent Soviet history:

> I think the political choice I made on joining the Communist party thirty years ago was correct. I have never been a political turncoat. I think that you can change the woman you love, but you must not change your political convictions. So I am, and shall remain, a

> member of the Communist party. . . . I am sure the party has a good
> future. The Communist idea is not dead, any more than socialism or
> the socialist ideal. After all, we have not spent a single day under
> socialism in the Leninist sense of the word. What we've had is the
> mirror-image of socialism, deformed socialism. . . . So it is too soon
> to say that the left-wing ideal is dead in the Soviet Union. As Mark
> Twain said, 'Rumours of my death have been greatly exaggerated.'

As a piece of political forecasting, Yanayev's assertions would win
few prizes. As an epitaph for the man who unwittingly destroyed
Communism in the USSR, they have an ironic resonance. But as
an indication of the fundamental devotion to a party and a political
ideal which seventy years of socialism had instilled in Communist
politicians, and which eventually pushed some of them to the
extremes of political folly to try to rescue that ideal, Yanayev's
remarks were illuminating and even touching.

Anatoly Lukyanov was a rather different proposition. Just as dedicated to the party as Yanayev, he was much more the Kremlin insider.
A self-confident, almost arrogant man, Lukyanov was constantly
accused of being overbearing and intolerant. His appointment as
Chairman of the Supreme Soviet had brought him great influence
which many deputies accused him of abusing. He was, they said,
adept at manipulating the parliamentary rule book to ensure that
votes always went the way he wanted; he would cut off speakers
who did not agree with his views and encourage those who did.
But Lukyanov had one trump card which virtually ensured his
political invulnerability: he was a close personal friend of Mikhail
Gorbachov. They had been at university together – Lukyanov
had been Gorbachov's superior in the college's Communist youth
organization – and they had remained close for forty years. We used
to refer to Lukyanov as Lucky Luke! (When it came to considering
his role in the coup, it was his personal betrayal of a lifelong friend
which was held against Lukyanov almost as much as his political
treachery.)

Since Gorbachov had come to power, he had kept Lukyanov
at his side. In March 1990 Gorbachov had vacated the position
of Chairman of the Supreme Soviet, the post whose holder had
always been styled 'President' of the Soviet Union, even though
it carried only nominal power compared to the real authority of
the Communist party General Secretaryship (which Gorbachov also
held). Having had himself appointed to the newly created and more
powerful position of executive State President, Gorbachov needed
to find a replacement for his old job. The choice was particularly

important, because the new electoral laws had created a Supreme
Soviet which was no longer docile and subservient like the old
parliament. Gorbachov needed someone he could trust to watch
over his interests in parliament now that he could no longer do
so personally. His choice of Lukyanov was unhesitating. As with
Yanayev, Gorbachov expressed his total trust in the man he was
nominating. As with Yanayev, he was again mistaken.

Lukyanov never overtly undermined Gorbachov's authority in
the Supreme Soviet, but reports began to emerge that he was
increasingly conniving with the hardline Soyuz ('Union') group of
deputies. Their manifesto was based almost solely on a belief in the
inviolability of the USSR, and a mission to keep the empire intact.
One of the Soyuz leaders, the half-Latvian Colonel Viktor Alksnis,
took me aside a month before the coup to explain the real goals of
his organization, and I kept a record of the conversation.

> Soyuz believes it is necessary to preserve the Soviet Union as a united
> federation. We have about 600 active supporters in the Congress of
> Peoples' Deputies, and 150 in the Supreme Soviet. . . . In December
> last year we demanded that Gorbachov produce a specific anti-crisis
> plan to save our country from economic catastrophe, political
> catastrophe and inter-ethnic catastrophe. Unfortunately Gorbachov
> proved unable to produce any anti-crisis plan, and that is the reason
> why we proposed a vote of no confidence in him. . . . Soyuz is united
> on the central issue: the need to preserve the USSR, and any measures –
> including extraordinary ones – are acceptable in order to save it. . . .

When pressed on whether the 'extraordinary measures' he was
advocating might include the use of military force against republics
wishing to secede and break up the Union, Alksnis replied that such
a step may be necessary.

While there was no evidence that Soyuz as an organization took
an active role in the putsch, many of its members were involved
on an individual basis; and the group's persistent hardline rhetoric
demanding the overthrow of the constitutionally appointed authorities helped to create the atmosphere of conservative dissatisfaction
which the coup leaders sought to exploit. Lukyanov's closeness to
a group like Soyuz, with its demands for the forcible preservation
of the Soviet Union and its contemptuous dismissal of Gorbachov's
weakness in letting republics break up the country, was ultimately
reflected in his involvement as the behind-the-scenes organizer of
the August coup. When I talked to him in July, he was already
making plain his dissatisfaction with Gorbachov's proposed Union
Treaty, which – in the eyes of the Soyuz group – was tantamount

to destroying the country they cherished and were dedicated to preserving.

Lukyanov's bland, modern office in the Supreme Soviet lacked the style and grandeur of Yanayev's apartments, but its book-lined walls spoke of the organized mind of a professional lawyer and a man used to rigid discipline. Exactly at the appointed time, he strode briskly into the office and shook hands. Compared to his reputation, his physical appearance was almost bathetic. Short and chubby with tufts of white hair on either side of a balding head, he peered short-sightedly through thick glasses designed to correct a pronounced squint in his left eye. He had attempted to stipulate in advance that certain topics could not be raised during our conversation, but I had refused to agree and the initial atmosphere was slightly frosty. Lukyanov, though, did the proper thing and offered coffee and biscuits; and I responded by picking what I thought to be an innocuous topic to open the conversation. How, I asked, did he see the future role of the Supreme Soviet once the Union Treaty had ben signed? The vehemence of his reply took me aback: 'The Supreme Soviet will preserve all the positive things from the current period and it will gain new qualities too. It will act as a rallying point for powers on an all-Union scale, and its scope after the Union Treaty will be only slightly affected . . . the powers of the Supreme Soviet will have to be reckoned with.'

The Union Treaty, with its proposals to reduce the power of the centre (and thus of the central organs like the Supreme Soviet), was clearly a sore point with Lukyanov, because he went on to list at great length the powers which would always remain with the centre and would never be ceded to the republics. 'These will cover the very important matters of international relations,' he said. 'Then there will be defence and security; there will also be the preservation and supervision of a single economic space on the basis of an integrated banking, customs and currency system. In addition, there are also the matters of transport and communications, energy, environmental safety . . .'

Lukyanov was particularly insistent that the centre must never cede control of taxation to the republics, seeing this as the key test of the viability of the Union: 'From my point of view, without federal taxation there can be no federation. In fact, the tax system and the federal tax were one of the causes of the American civil war between the Union states and the Confederate states. That's the reason why the problem has to be solved.'

Asked about Boris Yeltsin and his attempts to insist that laws passed by the republics take precedence over those enacted by the centre, Lukyanov almost spluttered with rage: 'If Yeltsin fails to honour the document which he signed, the Nine-plus-One declaration signed on the 23rd April, which says explicitly that Union laws have priority . . . Yelstsin must honour his signature agreeing that in the event of differences of opinion about the jurisdiction of laws of the Union and those of the republics, it is Union law that operates. . . . Pacts are made to be honoured.'

By now it was clear that Lukyanov was desperately clinging to elements of power which Gorbachov's Union Treaty was preparing to give away. Within a few days of my conversation with him, Lukyanov was to see further concessions in the treaty negotiations wipe out or seriously weaken virtually every element of central power he had so proudly mentioned. Yeltsin quickly declared that Russia would be taking at least some foreign policy responsibilities away from the central authorities by opening Russian embassies in foreign capitals alongside the existing Soviet missions, and would be aiming for separate UN membership; the republics were granted the right to form national guards, thus undermining the centre's monopoly on security concerns; the Baltics opened their own customs posts and several republics announced plans for their own currencies and banking systems, in direct contradiction of Lukyanov's demands for central control of economic levers; and, worst of all – in light of Lukyanov's insistence that the centre's dominant role in the imposition of taxation was a sine qua non for the very existence of the Union – Gorbachov proceeded to give away control of the tax system to the republican presidents, including Boris Yeltsin.

It was a series of reverses which Lukyanov must have regarded as the annihilation of all he had stood for in politics, and – like many other conservative-oriented members of the party – he must have felt a deep sense of betrayal. His political firmament had been cast down; his country was being broken up; his party was under threat; and the man behind all the noxious concessions was Mikhail Gorbachov, his long-time friend and party comrade. Under such conditions, Lukyanov's revolt and his desperate gamble on the coup become almost understandable.

If Yanayev joined the plot out of personal ambition, Lukyanov seems to have done so out of conviction. If Yanayev was thrust into the position of figurehead for the coup, that was because he happened to occupy the Vice-Presidency, the position on which ultimate power is automatically devolved if the President himself is incapacitated. Lukyanov, on the other hand, was the man who consciously took charge, organizing Yanayev, Yazov, Pugo, Pavlov and the others, pushing them into carrying through the gamble he had decided to take. When Lukyanov summoned Yanayev and Pavlov to the Kremlin to launch the coup, they were already half drunk after a series of vodka toasts at a party at Pavlov's dacha, and after the putsch was defeated Yanayev was found unconscious on his office floor surrounded by empty bottles. Pavlov was invalided out of the coup leadership because of 'hypertension', a favourite euphemism for alcoholic overindulgence. But Lukyanov remained composed and determined, never connecting himself publicly with the coup, but directing developments from behind the scenes. Deputies who visited him in his office at the Supreme Soviet during the putsch say he calmly rebuffed their expressions of concern, insisting that everything was under control.

If Yanayev, Pavlov and the others were adventurists, Lukyanov had the air of a man acting out of conviction. He gambled everything for a cause he seems to have believed in and, in the end, he lost.

4

The Gorbachov Factor

The simple, snap-shot view of the August coup, and one which at the time gained a certain currency in the West, was that the plotters were deluded fanatics, Communist dinosaurs trying to return the Soviet Union to its antediluvian past by overthrowing a popular regime of reformist liberals. Because the character and motives of the coup leaders in this version were so unrelievedly blackened, Mikhail Gorbachov was naturally depicted as playing the role of the man in the white hat.

I suggested in the previous chapter that the motives of the conspirators were slightly more complex than initial perceptions might allow, although in the final analysis their goal was – impossibly – to attempt to turn back the clock of history. But the snap-shot assessment of Gorbachov is much harder to sustain. By the summer of 1991 he was no longer the popular president he once had been; he was no longer leading the reform movement, and in many people's eyes he was simply being dragged along by it, or was even trying to slow it down.

For the whole of his six years in power, Gorbachov had been forced to walk a political tightrope between the competing demands of radicals and hardliners; between orthodox Communists on the one hand and reformers, both inside and outside the party, on the other; between the chauvinist, anti-capitalist old guard and the new thinkers who believed in rapprochement and cooperation with the West. To stay on the tightrope, Gorbachov had been forced to pander to the demands of both groups, to convince both political extremes that his programme was not a threat to their interests.

In the early part of his career in power, Gorbachov accomplished this with a certain panache. Constant cajoling and sleight of hand allowed him to convince the conservatives that his reforms were really in their interests, and to convince the liberals that his retreats from genuinely radical policies were only a tactical measure designed to ensure continued progress down the road of reform. But in the middle years of perestroika, he was forced into increasingly convoluted manoeuvres to keep his balance on the tightrope. This was the period in which his swings from right to left, from hardliners to radicals, became ever more violent, seemingly unpredictable and almost certainly out of his control. Then finally, in the late summer of 1991, Gorbachov's nimble footwork deserted him. He made one swing too many; he leaned too far to one side; he fell off the tightrope.

But why was the President of the USSR and the General Secretary of the Communist party forced into the humiliating position of having to obtain approval for his policy decisions from political interest groups? After all, no previous Soviet leader had had to do so. What were the processes which ultimately led to Gorbachov's stumble, to the August coup and to all its dramatic consequences? Could Gorbachov have prevented the coup if he had acted differently? And, perhaps the most important question of all, what were the historical pressures which led him to insist on appointing the eventual leaders of the coup to positions of great power, despite strident liberal warnings to him not to do so?

The polarization of conservatives and reformers has a long tradition in Russian political life, stretching back well before the 1917 revolution. The reformist tsars, Peter the Great, Catherine the Great and Aleksandr II, fought against the deep inertia of a country in their struggle to change it. By the mid-nineteenth century the same dichotomy had come to dominate intellectual and political life in the form of a constant, dynamic opposition between two philosophical camps, referred to as Westernizers and Slavophiles. The Westernizers were those who followed in Peter the Great's foot steps and accepted that Russia must learn from the west. Just as Peter had tried to pull Russia out of its backwardness and into the mainstream of European civilization, the Westernizers believed their country's future now lay in the adoption of economic, political and social ideas which had been tried and tested in the West. Unfortunately for the Westernizers, this approach necessarily involved the acceptance that foreign ideas were in some respects superior to the home grown equivalents, and this touched a raw nerve among the defenders of Russian pride. These were the Slavophiles, who expressed their opposition to anything Western, arguing that imported foreign values would not be appropriate to Russian conditions and could not lead to progress.

Instead, they propounded a doctrine of reliance on a Russian heritage, which they considered purer and more acceptable.

The opposition of Slavophiles and Westernizers permeated the culture of the period, forming a central theme in the novels of Turgenev and others, but it also contributed to the stifling of real reforms in the country. The same dichotomy persisted into the Soviet era, but now it found expression in a different way. Because the Bolsheviks had outlawed all political activity outside their own ranks, the split in ideas could not be formulated as a normal opposition of political parties or movements; and Stalin's campaign to wipe out 'factionalism' within the Communist party itself meant there could be little debate even within the ranks of those who held power. Stalin's practice of repressing opposition thought continued the tsarist authoritarian tradition, but also meant that Soviet leaders until the advent of Gorbachov operated largely within a monolithic system and were not faced by the need to adapt their policies to take account of conflicting political lobbies. But the ghost of the old Slavophile-Westernizer dichotomy resurfaced – not, this time, in the form of political opposition, but in the changes of course initiated by the party leadership itself.

The years of Soviet power have been characterized by the alternation of two different forms of the Communist model, which have been imposed successively since the revolution. When Lenin found the young Soviet state in serious economic difficulties in the early 1920s, his response was to relax the dogmatically rigid model of centralized control and state supremacy and to allow the re-emergence of certain elements of capitalism. This ideological swing was known as the New Economic Policy, or NEP. Individual enterprise was again tolerated within certain limits and Western investment was actively encouraged. A new breed of entrepreneurs known as NEPmen emerged, many growing rich in the new, freer conditions; and Western businessmen arrived in Russia to renew old links which had been broken during the revolution. The NEP was, in effect, an echo of the Westernising tradition of tsarist times.

The advent of Stalin brought a violent swing back in the direction of what might earlier have have been equated with Slavophilism, and which now earned the description of War Communism. It was based, in effect, on the premise that the USSR was alone, and was surrounded by actual or potential enemies in the capitalist world. Most foreign investment links were severed and social or political concepts deemed to be of foreign origin were abandoned. This meant the reversal of the quasi-capitalist reforms introduced under the NEP and the destruction of the nascent class of independent businessmen. Agriculture was collectivized and peasants who had shown any inclination to profit from personal initiative (the so-called *kulaks*) were deported or shot. The country was put on a siege footing; literature, music and the arts were silenced or put at the service of the state, and the excesses of War Communism were allowed to define the character of Soviet political practice for the next three decades until Stalin's death.

Further experiments with the more liberal, reformist version of socialism reappeared under Khrushchev and again with Kosygin's economic revisions in 1965. Gorbachov's initial vision of change was directly in the tradition of these past attempts at reform. He repeatedly invoked the example of Lenin's NEP to justify the economic relaxation he was proposing, and all the evidence suggests that he at first intended his policies to have only the same limited effect as the previous changes of direction (in other words, to liberalize and improve the Communist economic system, but not to change its political structures in any irrevocable way).

The qualitative difference between the Gorbachov reforms and those of the past, however, was glasnost. While previous leaders had liberalized, they had done it within the scope of the monolithic structure. They had not destroyed the party's monopoly on power or its right to make unchallenged political decisions. Khrushchev had, in effect, imposed liberal reform using the powers of a dictator. Gorbachov, though, sought to introduce change with the cooperation of the people; and to do that, he had to unleash the people's right to speak. The people were effectively asked, 'Do you want to keep the same old unsuccessful system we have inherited; or do you want the new vision of change which I, your leader, am offering you?' But instead of replying to that limited question, one section of the people used their new right to speak to propose a third option: 'We don't want the old system,' they replied, 'but neither do we want your circumscribed version of reform. We want total and radical change.'

Gorbachov initially invoked the force of popular opinion to help him dislodge those who were opposed to any form of change in the Soviet Union, but in doing so he gave public voice to the opposing political forces which had lain dormant under previous Soviet leaders. He found that his concept of reform could no longer simply be imposed on the country, but that he now had to reckon with competing demands from both ends of the spectrum for their views to be taken into account. His early decision on glasnost had set in train the process which would keep him under pressure throughout his period in power and would ultimately take power away from him.

The opposing forces of reform and conservatism, whose influence in Soviet society had in the past alternated in cycles lasting decades, now began to battle for prominence on an almost daily basis. The first years of Gorbachov's reign were the period of 'phoney perestroika', where talk of plans for change was little more than a device to test the prevailing political mood. Gorbachov's own vision of reform at that time seemed to be based on the teachings of his old mentor Yuri Andropov, focussing less on an extension of democracy than on the need for greater discipline and integrity, both from the leadership and from the people. His first speech as General Secretary to party officials in April 1985 specifically endorsed Andropov's concept of greater financial independence for enterprises and factories, but maintained the centralized control over the economy inherited from Stalinist times; and the programme adopted at the April 23rd central committee plenum failed to endorse specific targets for reforming the economic system. Gorbachov's first public campaign also carried the Andropov stamp: the tough anti-drink measures introduced in 1985 were designed to combat alcoholism, absenteeism and idustrial inefficiency, but took little notice of public opinion, which was strongly opposed. The restrictions on alcohol were later quietly phased out, but were only recently officially declared a mistake.

Throughout 1985, though, Gorbachov was advancing liberal allies to positions of power. Aleksandr Yakovlev became head of the Central Committee's propaganda department in August; Eduard Shevardnadze was made Foreign Minister in July; and Boris Yeltsin took over as Moscow party chief in December. While opposition to reform remained strong at home, Gorbachov's most radical proposals were restricted to his foreign policy. A series of dramatic offers on arms reduction resulted in a summit meeting with Ronald Reagan in Geneva in November, which set a timetable for further meetings in the future; while the first indications that Gorbachov was moving towards a decision to withdraw from Afghanistan followed eight months later.

Both the Afghan decision and the arms cut proposals, though, were partially dictated by Moscow's need to reduce its military budget in order to release funds to tackle the crisis in the civilian economy (the prime cause, many would argue, for the flirtation with reform in the first place), and it was not until the end of 1986 that Gorbachov began to go beyond the bounds of what previous refomist leaders had attempted. In statements made in the first half of that year, Gorbachov had publicly defended the continuing internal exile of nuclear physicist and dissident Andrei Sakharov. Sakharov, he said, had committed 'illegal acts', and had been properly punished. But in December 1986 Gorbachov began to prove his genuine liberal intent: he made a personal phone call to Sakharov at his place of exile in Gorky and invited him and his wife Elena Bonner to return to Moscow. After six years of internal exile, Sakharov – the country's enduring voice of conscience – had been restored, and it was Gorbachov who had to take the credit.

With the Sakharov release, the image of Gorbachov as a liberal reformer prepared to push the frontiers of change further than any leader in the past began to take on a credibility it had previously lacked. But what the Sakharov release also made clear was the extent of the conservative opposition Gorbachov was now facing. Reports of the deliberate obstruction of Gorbachov's policies by hardline members of the apparat – the Communist bureaucracy which controlled all areas of Soviet life and which could foil policy initiatives simply by refusing to act on them – were becoming rife. As early as September, a Central Committee resolution had complained of the slow progress of perestroika and had named individual ministries which it said were hindering the implementation of reforms. By early 1987 Gorbachov was publicly calling on workers to support his initiatives against party bureaucrats who tried to oppose them. In a speech to the Trades Union Congress in Moscow, he talked openly of disputes within the top party leadership over the pace of reform, and confirmed that the repeated delays in calling a Central Committee plenum had been due to disagreements over the reformist platform he was intending to put forward.

Gorbachov's first response to conservative opposition seems to have been to meet them head on. During the course of 1986–87 scores of writers and poets, previously considered anti-Soviet, were widely printed for the first time in the USSR, including Boris Pasternak, Vladimir Nabokov, Nikolai Gumilyov and Vladimir Vysotsky. Jamming of the BBC Russian Service was ended. Reformist editors were appointed to leading newspapers and journals, and films like the anti-Stalinist, Christian allegory *Repentance* were shown for the first time.

But Gorbachov was soon forced to take the conservative threat more seriously. In a meeting with representatives of Soviet newspapers and the broadcast media, he pledged that glasnost would continue but he also felt it necessary to reassure supporters of orthodox Communism that this would not be allowed to damage their interests. Soon afterwards, Yegor Ligachov made a speech which was seen as a rallying call for conservative opposition to perestroika. Ligachov was the Politburo member responsible for ideology and thus considered the number two in the party leadership. As such, he was the conservatives' most highly placed spokesman and the man assumed to be leading the resistance to reform (although a curious reluctance to ditch the old party pretence of unanimity at the highest levels meant that even those most opposed to change continued to mouth their enthusiastic loyalty to perestroika; and the refomers in the highest echelons equally refused to identify publicly the men who were standing in their way).

In his speech in the city of Saratov, Ligachov claimed that the 'period of stagnation' (the catch word for the Brezhnev years, now condemned by the Gorbachovites as typifying the worst aspects of old-style Communism) should not be totally condemned. In a clear expression of dissatisfacion over the pace of reform, he said the Brezhnev era had produced some positive achievements, and that these should be praised, not denounced.

At the January plenum Gorbachov had tested the water for his plans to introduce limited democratic reforms, suggesting the unprecedented idea of multi-candidate elections held by secret ballot. At this stage, he proposed the use of such procedures only for the election of factory managers and the directors of enterprises. But the conservatives rightly saw it as the thin end of the wedge, and staged an elaborate blocking campaign. With Gorbachov now fully aware of the importance of keeping the hardliners appeased, the idea was held in abeyance, to resurface at a more opportune moment. In his Revolution Day speech, similar concerns led him to make only a mild denunciation of Stalinism and to defend the Molotov-Ribbentrop pact as having been necessary for Soviet strategic purposes.

Gorbachov's softer line towards the conservatives, though, soon brought him outspoken enemies from the other end of the spectrum. At a closed door Central Committee plenum in October 1987, the fiery liberal Boris Yeltsin launched a biting critique of the conservatives, which targeted Gorbachov as well as Ligachov. Amid stormy scenes, Yeltsin's request to resign as a candidate member of the Politburo was accepted and two weeks later he was publicly pilloried by Gorbachov and removed as Moscow party boss. The incident set the battle lines for the future political balance, with Gorbachov now being sniped at by Ligachov and his supporters from the right and by Yeltsin and the radicals from the left. The Soviet leader now had to look over both shoulders as he tried to keep his balance on the tightrope.

Gorbachov's announcement in February 1988 of a total withdrawal from Afghanistan sparked anger among the old guard, and the first serious attempt to undermine the General Secretary's position. With Gorbachov out of the country on a visit to Yugoslavia, the newspaper *Sovietskaya Rossiya* published what amounted to a manifesto for hardline resistance to perestroika. Presented as a letter from a teacher in Leningrad by the name of Nina Andreeva, it was entitled 'I cannot foresake my principles', and it summed up the discontent felt by the millions of othodox Communists who regarded perestroika as an abomination. Nina Andreeva's attack on liberal reformers, printed in an official state newspaper, was seen as a signal from the highest authorities that the day of the reformers was over. Ligachov's role in the affair was darkly hinted at by several sources at *Sovietskaya Rossiya*: as Gorbachov's de facto deputy, he was in charge of Politburo meetings during the General Secretary's travels abroad, and there was speculation that he was using his boss's absence to strengthen his own position with a possible bid for power in mind. It took more than three weeks before *Pravda* published a rebuttal of Nina Andreeva, and confirmed that Gorbachov had come out on top – for the moment at least – in the power struggle going on behind the scenes.

In the months leading up to the summer of 1988 Gorbachov clearly reached the decision that the discontent of the conservatives in the Communist party (where they still commanded strong support and were threatening a revolt) represented a real threat to his own position. He was ruling the USSR in his capacity of General Secretary of the Communist party, a position to which the party had appointed him and from which the party could remove him. What he needed was to widen his power base, to win a mandate to rule from a source which would be less likely or less able to cast him off. At the time Gorbachov seemingly believed his stock was higher among the liberals and among the ordinary Soviet people than it was among the hardliners in the party. In one of the deft pieces of footwork which were his stock in trade, Gorbachov announced to the 19th Party Conference in July that the Soviet Union would henceforth have a new parliamentary and presidential system. In order to give the new President a semblance of democratic legitimacy without actually having to run in national elections, Gorbachov devised a cunning scheme. There would be an enhanced parliament, called the Congress of People's Deputies, to be elected partially by free national ballot. The Congress, which would meet once or twice a year, would appoint a smaller body from its own members, which would sit as a semi-permanent national parliament. Although it would be known by the existing name of Supreme Soviet, it was expected to be very different from the old rubber-stamp parliament which bore that title. Before dissolving, the Congress of People's Deputies would elect a Chairman, who would also be the head of state, and generally referred to as President. The key element, though, was that the new incumbent would take over most of the powers previously enjoyed by the leader of the Communist party, including control of foreign policy, security and defence; overall responsibility for the adoption of new legislation; economic strategy and the right to nominate the Prime Minister. The chosen candidate – whom everyone assumed would be Gorbachov – could hold the office of Communist Party General Secretary simultaneously, but there was no doubting which post would carry the real authority. And the advantage for Gorbachov was that he could henceforth be removed from the post only by the whole parliament. This meant that he could not suffer the same fate as Khrushchev, who was sacked as Communist leader (and consequently as leader of the country) by a clique of hardliners within the party elite.

Despite some misgivings, the Conference accepted Gorbachov's ideas in principle, many of the conservative delegates believing they could later block the proposals by the usual methods of red tape and delay. But Gorbachov pulled off a master stroke: at the very end of the Conference, when delegates were preparing to go home and were off their guard, he pulled from his pocket a crumpled piece of paper and said in a very matter of fact way, 'By the way, comrades, I have the timetable for my proposals here. Shall we vote now to accept it?' Without fully understanding what they were letting themselves in for, the delegates almost automatically raised their hands in favour. Gorbachov thanked them and declared the Conference closed. Only later did it become clear what they had voted to accept: the Soviet

Union's first multi-candidate elections would take place in March the following year, and the resulting parliament would meet to elect a new President immediately afterwards. The Communist party had in effect just voted to loosen its own grip on the levers of power in the USSR.

The election campaign for the Congress of Deputies in the first half of 1989 did more than any other event to unleash the previously repressed force of Soviet public opinion. It was the essential watershed which marked the transition from 'phoney perestroika' to the real thing. Now it was clear that Gorbachov was serious about reform: he was not just tinkering with the system like his predecessors, he had changed the system. Indeed, once he had given the people their head, there was little way he could ever turn back. From that point forward, the pace of change was no longer being dictated from above, but from below – by the Soviet people.

The elections were initially called by Gorbachov as a means to create a countervailing force for reform, intended to balance out the force of the conservatives, who until then had been the biggest threat to him and his vision of limited democratic change. But the fervour unleashed among the population by those election campaigns was something no one could have predicted. My memories of those months, of the massive public rallies in the car park of the Luzhniki football stadium, addressed by Sakharov, Yeltsin, Stankevich, Popov and all the future stars of the liberal movement, convinced me for the first time that some form of popular democracy had arrived in the Soviet Union and that it would now be very difficult to root it out.

The expression on the people's faces proved it more than anything: years of pent-up thirst for information, for participation, and for the chance really to change things in their own country had come to be slaked at the well of democracy. Every activist who had a pile of poltical tracts to distribute was immediately surrounded by hundreds of hands grasping and fighting to read his views; every speaker, however esoteric, was carefully listened to, discussed, applauded or booed with the enthusiasm of a nation which had finally discovered the excitement and joy of an unfettered right to public existence. It was the springtime of their political awakening, and people still had implicit faith in the worth of what they were fighting for. The fervour was naive and genuine, and the cynicism of disappointment (which was to infuse the Soviet political scene for the latter half of 1990 and the first half of 1991) was still a long way off. It was not even as if the elections were fully open or fair: one third of the seats in the Congress were being reserved for appointees who would generally toe the Communist line. But the men and women who were standing for election to the contested seats knew perfectly well that they were about to put their foot in the door of parliamentary democracy, and that once it was opened neither the Communists nor anyone else would easily be able to close it again.

Gorbachov had hoped the elections would create a new, controllable force that he could play off against his old hardline foes. But in the event, he got more than he had bargained for. In Moscow, Leningrad, Kiev and Minsk, party officials were humiliated at the ballot box: even where they insisted on standing as unopposed candidates, enough people took the trouble to cross out their names to deny them the necessary fifty per cent of the vote. And a protest vote against the Communist party was also, by definition, a protest vote against the General Secretary of that party, the man who had given the people the chance to vote in the first place, Mikhail Gorbachov. In independence-minded republics, separatist movements had a field day: the Lithuanian Sajudis won 31 of the republic's 42 seats; in Latvia the Popular Front won 25 out of 29; and in Estonia they picked up 15 out of 21. Perhaps most worrying of all for Gorbachov, his most powerful radical critic, Boris Yeltsin, swept the board across the whole of Moscow with ninety per cent of the votes cast. For Gorbachov, the lesson of the 1989 elections was that his most powerful potential opponent would no longer be the hardliners in the Communist party, but the radicals who wanted to go further and faster with reform than he was prepared to allow. This new force, Gorbachov might ruefully have reflected, was created partially by his own efforts. But by then it was too late, and he could do little else but adjust his balance and continue walking his tight-rope.

He might have helped his own cause if he had reacted more sensitively to the lessons the elections seemed to be offering. He could have thrown in his lot with the liberals by making an early exit from his post of Communist Party leader; which would have saved him from sharing the stigma of the party's defeat at the ballot boxes, and could have seized the chance to move down the road the newly elected radicals were asking him to follow. But three days after the elections Gorbachov was half-heartedly justifying the party for its poor showing, and stating his opposition to the very concept of a multi-party system in the Soviet Union. Under our conditions, he said, that would be 'absurd'.

Despite his rift with the Ligachovs of the party, Gorbachov was still evidently the prisoner of his Communist past. He was showing an inability to break with the party that formed and nurtured him, a blind, emotional attachment to his political roots which was to serve him ill when it came to the difficult political choices he would have to make in the aftermath of the August 1991 coup.

In May 1989 the newly elected Congress of People's Deputies met in the Kremlin for its inaugural session. It was a more diverse and more radical parliament than any in the Soviet Union's history, but a large number of the deputies were, nonetheless, from the old guard: 750 of the 2250 seats were filled by appointees of 'public organizations' (all of which were, by definition, licensed by the Communist party), and a certain proportion of the others were occupied by conservatives elected in their own right. The 542 deputies chosen by the Congress to form the smaller, standing parliament (the Supreme Soviet) reflected the same political complexion.

The vote to name Gorbachov as Chairman (that is, to make him state president) went according to plan; but in the minds of many liberals, doubts remained. The reason Gorbachov had given for the introduction of the new parliamentary and presidential system was to create a 'law-governed state', ruled by authorities which were responsible to the people: the Congress had been elected by the people, in a way that the old Communist *apparatchiks* who used to run the country never were. But Gorbachov himself had faced no democratic scrutiny: he had been named as one of the party's guaranteed nominees to the Congress of Deputies (100 candidates for 100 seats), and he had been appointed President by the Congress, not the nation. Many liberals were asking why the man who advocated democracy did not feel able to take part in its fundamental processes.

A month later, when the new Supreme Soviet convened, liberal discontent with Gorbachov surfaced for the first time in a legislative body. Several of the President's nominees for posts in the new government were rejected by the parliament, including the man he wanted as Deputy Prime Minister. The toughest fight was over the appointment of the Defence Minister. Gorbachov was backing Dmitri Yazov, who had held the post since May 1987; but the liberals viewed Yazov as a hardliner and a potential enemy of reform in the Soviet Union. The President, though, was insistent. As he was later to do with Gennady Yanayev, Gorbachov made repeated declarations of support for Yazov, assuring the deputies that the Marshal was a 'progressive' who deserved their backing, and as with Yanayev, he even resorted to bending the rules to get his man elected. Normally, an absolute majority of the 542 members of the parliament was needed to confirm a government minister, but Gorbachov, seeing in advance that Yazov was not going to get this, produced a little sleight of hand, asking the hall to agree that Yazov could be appointed simply by a majority of the deputies present in the chamber, a considerably lower figure. It was an outrageous disregard for parliamentary practice, but by his action Gorbachov saved Yazov's bacon. The Marshal got 256 votes, which was 16 fewer than he would have needed for an absolute majority, but just enough to scrape the fifty per cent of those present that Gorbachov had pleaded for.

History, of course, later revealed that Gorbachov won the appointment of a man who in August 1991 would order the army to overthrow him. He did the same thing with Yanayev, and he personally oversaw the political advancement of Lukyanov. The other coup leaders, Pavlov, Pugo and the rest, also owed their appointments to Gorbachov's recommendation. In virtually every instance there had been prominent liberal voices warning loudly against giving such men access to the levers of power. Some had explicitly spoken of the increased dangers of a military coup with such people in the Kremlin; and when the coup happened there was a cacophony of reproach against Gorbachov for his folly in trusting them. By throwing in his lot with the men who were later to send the tanks onto the streets, said the liberals in retrospect, Gorbachov was just as responsible for the putsch as the men who ordered it.

Gorbachov's supporters argued that he was forced to go along with hardline pressures to a certain extent (and that included the presence of old guard politicians in his government) because to provoke an open confrontation with the conservatives would have endangered the whole of his reform programme. The radicals argued that Gorbachov did too little to oppose the influence of the hardliners. The cynics argued that Gorbachov was and always had been a hardliner himself: although he concealed it under a mask of reformist platitudes, ran the argument, he had always been dedicated to the triumph of the Communist party, and any changes he made in society were designed only to strengthen Communist dominance in the long term.

This third scenario, which explains the advancement of hardliners as the natural inclination of a hardline president, was persuasively argued to me by the radical Moscow politician Arkady Murashov. But it fails to account for the real shift of political power Gorbachov effected away from the Communist party and in favour of state organs, including a directly elected parliamentary body. Of the two remaining explanations, it remains a moot point whether Gorbachov's passivity in face of hardline pressure was the result of weakness, or the necessary consequence of a long-term strategy to balance off the two political extremes and ensure the ultimate triumph of a moderate but workable reform programme that could be introduced without provoking social confrontation.

At the Congress of Deputies in May 1989, the radical mayor of Leningrad, Anatoly Sobchak, had quietly buttonholed Gorbachov after a particularly stormy session and appealed to the President to take more decisive action against the hardliners. Sobchak recounts that Gorbachov paused for a moment, and then replied: 'You are arguing from the point of view of Moscow or Leningrad, the big cities where the population wants liberal reform. If I only had to deal with Moscow or Leningrad, then I could press ahead with reforms much faster, but don't forget that I have to deal with the whole of the Soviet Union.' And Sobchak says that he realized that Gorbachov was right. There were – and probably still are – millions of people in the conservative countryside, the backward towns and villages, who did not want radical changes in their lives and would fight against them. And it is in that historical perspective that Gorbachov's appointment of conservative politicians to posts of responsibility must be viewed.

In the summer of 1989, following the Yazov debacle, liberal opposition to Gorbachov became more organized and more influential. A new movement of radical deputies in the Congress was formed under the title of the Inter-Regional Group. Led by men like Andrei Sakharov, Boris Yeltsin, Gavriil Popov and the outspoken historian Yuri Afanasyev, the movement provided a focus for liberals whose declared aim was to press Gorbachov into root and branch democratization. Under Article 6 of the Soviet constitution, which enshrined the leading role of the Communists, other political parties were in effect banned, so the Inter-Regional Group was prevented from formally declaring itself a new party. Their response was a concerted campaign to get Article 6 abolished.

A series of demonstrations culminated in an unprecedented campaign of political strikes towards the end of the year. These were largely the result of Andrei Sakharov's pressure for an early end to the Communist monopoly of power, but despite Sakharov's urging, the strikes were poorly supported and fizzled out. They did, though, alarm Gorbachov, who showed his concern over the growing pressure from the liberals in a meeting with leading newspaper editors in the Kremlin. Gorbachov attacked the 'irresponsible and inflammatory' statements of Afanasyev, Popov and others and called the Inter-Regional Group a 'band of gangsters'. In an outburst of nervous fury, he demanded the resignation of those newspaper editors who had supported the radicals' demands, singling out Vladislav Starkov of the popular *Argumenty i Fakty* journal for particularly vituperative attention.

Starkov told me afterwards that he had never seen Gorbachov so angry, and he suggested the outburst was a reflection of the President's alienation from the liberals and his coming swing towards the conservatives. The radicals had tried to push Gorbachov further than he was ready to go, or further than his hardline colleagues would let him go. It was now becoming questionable whether Gorbachov was in control of his balancing act between left and right, or whether he was simply being swept backwards and forwards by inimical political forces. (Starkov himself was fortunate: his fellow journalists were determined to make the matter an issue of principle, and they threatened to close the paper down if Starkov bowed to Gorbachov's demands. In the end, Starkov kept his job and Gorbachov's threat to dismiss him was quietly forgotten.)

Andrei Sakharov's death on 14 December 1989 came at the height of the liberals' campaign for the abolition of Article 6, and it seems to have wrought a temporary truce between the president and the radicals. Gorbachov took a public role in Sakharov's funeral, paying tribute to the former dissident's contribution to reform. By the following month, he was already suggesting that he would not oppose the removal of the Communist power monopoly, and when a quarter of a million people demonstrated outside the Kremlin in early February Gorbachov's mind was already made up. He had accepted that Article 6 would have to go, and he had actively encouraged the mass demonstration to put pressure on potential hardline opponents of the decision. The following day, at a plenum of the party's Central Committee, he proposed the abolition of the reference in the constitution to the leading role of Communism in the USSR, thus opening the way for a multi-party system. The proposals were adopted after fierce debate and threats from the Communist old guard. But the fact that Gorbachov got the measures through was again testimony to his poltical acumen. He had chosen the right moment and had mollified the right people to ensure the passage of a bill which changed the political face of the Soviet Union.

In March 1990, though, Gorbachov disappointed the liberals yet again. He had proposed changes in the role of the presidency which would give the post wide-ranging executive powers: the new presidency would emulate the French and American systems, and the net effect would be virtually to remove the influence of the CPSU General Secretary in the running of the country. The radicals understood this and gave their backing to the move. But instead of standing for election in a national poll, as the radicals were demanding, Gorbachov had himself reappointed as President by a session of the Congress of People's Deputies. Doubts about Gorbachov's democratic credentials surfaced once again. Gorbachov justified his decision by saying the country needed urgent measures and there was no time to lose in an election campaign. But the end result was that Gorbachov wasted what was probably his last chance to win a democratic mandate in the Soviet Union. In March 1990 he still retained a measure of popularity among the people, and his liberal support had been boosted by the decision to abolish Article 6. But within months his standing had plummeted and opinion polls from that time onwards have shown he would gain only minimal support in a national election.

On May Day that year Gorbachov was booed and jeered as he stood on the Lenin mausoleum watching the parade. The main heckling came from an organized detachment of Yeltsin supporters who had joined the end of the official workers' parade and were, astoundingly, allowed to march right into Red Square and under the noses of the Politburo. Their shouted complaints to Gorbachov were that he had sold out to the conservatives and had begun to block reform instead of promoting it; and it was this heckling from the 'left' as Russians term it (that is, from the radicals) which led Gorbachov to stalk off the mausoleum. But there were also attacks from the 'right' that May Day, with hardliners and Stalinists also infiltrating the parade and booing Gorbachov for having sold out to the liberals. The President was quite evidently under fire from both ends of the political spectrum, and each of the political extremes clearly believed he had sold out to their enemies. Gorbachov himself had earlier taken the line that if both conservatives and radicals were criticizing him, then he must be taking the right path. But by this stage of his career in power, he seems to have become obsessed with reconciling the extremes and with trying to please everyone at the same time. It was a characteristic which was later to paralyse Soviet economic policy, when Gorbachov vainly tried to merge two mutually exclusive economic plans.

In political terms, Gorbachov's temporizing had left him almost friendless, and in the second half of 1990 and the first months of 1991 he changed his team of advisers with alarming frequency from liberals to conservatives and back again. But May Day 1990 can be seen in retrospect as marking the beginning of Gorbachov's two final switches in political direction, each one of them more pronounced and more turbulent than ever before, and each seeming at the time to be final and irrevocable.

His major policy shift in the latter part of 1990 was in the direction of the hardliners. There may have been psychological reasons for it (he was clearly stung by the radicals' attacks on him during May Day: a new law laying down punishments of up to six years in jail for 'insulting the honour of the President' was introduced less than two weeks after his humiliation on the mausoleum), but the effects of the President's new mood were soon felt. At the 28th Communist party Congress in July, Boris Yeltsin and his allies announced that they could no longer remain members of the party, and walked out in a dramatic show of protest. Expectations had been aroused that Gorbachov might use the moment to renounce his leadership of the party and throw in his lot with the radicals. But instead he allowed himself to be renominated and took the decision to stay in a party which had lost its liberal wing and was looking increasingly out of touch with the pace of reform.

An agreement to cooperate with Yeltsin over plans to revitalize the Soviet economy ended in recriminations when Gorbachov reneged on his promises to support radical market-oriented measures, and in October Yeltsin announced that his Russian republic would proceed with the measures in spite of Gorbachov's refusal. Two weeks later Gorbachov responded with legislation asserting that laws issued by the central, Soviet authorities must take precedence over laws issued by the republics. Within a day, Yeltsin hit back with his own, Russian legislation declaring that

Russian law would take precedence, and the so called 'war of laws' broke out.

It was an undisguised power struggle between the reformist republics which wanted to press ahead with economic liberalization and the centre which remained much more cautious. It spread, too, into a clash with the separatist Baltic states, which was eventually to result in the massacres in Vilnius and Riga in the new year. Because the republics were pushing so hard for reform, and because Gorbachov was resisting them, he was forced into a position that became increasingly authoritarian and repressive. At the end of November, he made use of the emergency powers he had claimed for himself at the Congress of People's Deputies to issue a series of presidential decrees. The first of these introduced measures to boost the powers of the army. Because of recent harrassment of Soviet troops, said Gorbachov (there had been anti-Red Army demonstrations in the Baltics), soldiers would henceforth be empowered to defend themselves and their property by using their weapons. Formulated at the same time but only announced two months later was a decree to begin joint army and police patrols of all major cities. The reason given was the rise in crime rates, but many feared it was another potentially repressive measure to stifle political opposition on the streets.

The hand of Gorbachov's hardline colleagues in the Soviet leadership was unmistakeable in these measures. The decrees on the army were announced on national television not by Gorbachov himself, but by Defence Minister Yazov. And in early December the KGB chief Vladimir Kryuchkov appeared on the screen to make a long and rambling speech full of the sort of rhetoric which had not been heard since the Brezhnev years. There was, said Kryuchkov, a growing danger to the Soviet motherland: anti-Communist elements had stirred up rioting and revolt. But, he added, the KGB would fight these elements and their backers from abroad with all the means at its disposal.

The atmosphere was being prepared for the crack-down in the Baltics and Gorbachov was making no overt attempt to halt the slide into repression. The running, it is true, was being made by the hardliners surrounding him, but Gorbachov was at the very least a passive participant.

On 2 December, he announced that he was sacking his Interior Minister Vadim Bakatin. The news was greeted with shock and dismay. Bakatin was a Communist, but he had always been considered to be on the party's most reformist wing. He had distinguished himself by his support for the 'rule of law' (in other words, by his fight against the abuse of power and the incorrect use of legal sanctions to repress political dissent) and he had become, like Eduard Shevardnadze, a hero of reformers and democrats. Gorbachov gave no public reason for firing Bakatin, although it took little imagination to guess that it was in response to pressure from men like Yazov and Kryuchkov. Gorbachov himself later hinted as much, and did his best to bring Bakatin back into public life.

But it was the new men appointed to head the Interior Ministry, and to control the 400,000 special interior troops at their disposal, who gave the biggest cause for alarm. Boris Pugo had previously been KGB chief in his native Latvia and had won a reputation for fierce opposition to nationalist aspirations in the Baltics. If the Kremlin strong men were planning to move against the separatists, he was an ideal member of the team. As his deputy, Pugo got Boris Gromov, the former commander of Soviet forces in Afghanistan and now an undisguisedly hardline member of the Congress of Deputies. (I had met Gromov in Afghanistan two years earlier and was struck by his cruelly ruthless attitude to the rebel Mujehadin guerrillas: the thought of such a personality being turned on the civilian population of the USSR was worrying in the extreme.) By appointing Boris Pugo, Gorbachov had now completed the team of men who would move to oust him in August 1991.

In early December Aleksandr Yakovlev wrote an article for the newspaper *Moskovsky Komsomolets* in which he warned: 'The conservative and reactionary forces, mercilessly seeking revenge, have mounted an offensive. I am deeply disturbd by the inertia . . . of the forces of democracy.' The warning was taken up with greater impact by Eduard Shevardnadze on 20 December, when his astonishing speech of resignation to the Congress of Deputies revealed to the world what had been going behind the scenes: 'The reformers have gone into hiding. A dictatorship is approaching. I tell you this with full responsibility. No one knows what this dictatorship will be like, what kind of dictator will come to power. . . . I am resigning . . . Let this be my contribution, my protest against the onset of dictatorship.'

A long personal friendship stopped Shevardnadze implicating Gorbachov directly in the plans for dictatorship, but he left little doubt that he felt the President had not acted firmly enough to avert the threat: 'I would like to express my sincere gratitude to Mikhail Sergeevich Gorbachov. I am his friend. I am a fellow thinker . . . We did great work in international affairs. But I think it is my duty to resign. As a man, as a citizen, as a Communist, I cannot reconcile myself to what is happening in my country and to the trials which await our people'.

Shevardnadze never returned to the close relationship he had previously enjoyed with Gorbachov: their quarrel over the hardline shift of the Soviet leadership during the winter of 1990 had been too deep and acrimonious ever to be forgotten, and when Shevardnadze was invited to become a member of Gorbachov's new team of advisers after the August coup he – and Aleksandr Yakovlev – refused with disdain. (In Spring 1990, eight months before his resignation speech, Shevardnadze had concluded a similar warning about the threat of a hardline revolt by saying: 'Consequently, we must act to avoid dictatorship. We must support those who oppose dictatorship, especially Gorbachov, who began perestroika.' By December his references to Gorbachov had become much more ambiguous, suggesting at least a suspicion that the President had sold out to the conservatives.) The subsequent events in Lithuania and Latvia bore out the truth of Shevardnadze's warning and provided the immediate fruits of Gorbachov's flirtation with the hardliners.

Gorbachov himself gave various explanations for his change of political orientation, for what the liberal writer Ales Adamovich called the 'process of surrounding the President with colonels and generals . . . surrounding him and making him a hostage'. In the immediate aftermath of Shevardnadze's resignation, Gorbachov muttered that the leadership was 'moving to the right because society is moving to the right'. His most liberal aides earnestly reported that the flirtation with the hard men was merely a temporary arrangement, necessary to get the country through the winter. Others talked of the growing unrest in the republics which was threatening the survival of the reforms Gorbachov was committed to, and hinted that he had entered a marriage of convenience with the KGB and the army: they were necessary to him as the only means available to keep order. Even the dismissed Vadim Bakatin told me that he was convinced Gorbachov was still committed to the ultimate goal of democratization, but that he had to make some strategic adjustments on the way: he was forced by prevailing circumstances to make sacrifices (among them, his devoted Interior Minister), but that these were all temporary measures. Gorbachov would, he claimed, return to the true path of perestroika in the end. But some observers were suggesting that Gorbachov's only remaining purpose was to hold on to power, and that he had sold his soul to the hardline devils to do so.

Whatever the reasons for Gorbachov's swing to the conservatives during the winter of 1990–91, whether it was through weakness or a self-seeking lust for power, or part of a long-term strategy to salvage perestroika from a particularly difficult period in its development, his conduct did undeniably strengthen the position of the reactionary forces. His own actions had brought Yanayev, Lukyanov and Yazov to power; Pugo was foisted on him because he had shown he had no inclination to resist. So when Gorbachov finally made his last great change of direction in the spring and summer of 1991, the damage had already been done.

As was pointed out in the previous chapter, Gorbachov's putative reconciliation with the liberals – his agreement to the new Union Treaty reducing the traditional powers of the centre, and his proposed cooperation with Boris Yeltsin – could not be consummated before the hardliners rallied their forces and staged the August coup; and in the final analyis, it was Gorbachov who was to blame. His actions during the winter had left the conservatives with so much influence in the top echelons of power that he could never realistically expect to desert them for the liberals without provoking a backlash. In the end, the hardliners were hoist with their own petard, and the very policies they had attempted to overthrow ultimately triumphed. But Gorbachov was not to know that in advance, and history's assessment of his role in the process which led to the coup is unlikely be a flattering one.

5

The Role of the Army

In February 1989, on one of the coldest days of a Russian winter where temperatures were regularly hitting minus thirty, a small crowd huddled together outside Moscow's Olympic Stadium. On a makeshift platform, a bulky man with the bearing and clipped tones of a Soviet army officer was speaking through a megaphone, stamping his feet either in anger or simply trying to keep warm as he roared his message to the steaming bodies before him.

The man was Vitaly Urashchev, a colonel in the army reserve, and the new leader of an unprecedented organization within the Soviet armed forces. Urashchev had just been elected as head of Shchit, the first ever independent trade union for Soviet soldiers, sailors and airmen. Shchit is the Russian word for 'shield', and the union's first declared priority was the protection of servicemen's rights, a campaign which was just beginning to lead them into such grey areas as the defence of soldiers who had been victimized for their political views. But what Urashchev was telling those willing to listen amid the Moscow snow that day was of much more immediate importance: 'I have to tell you,' he shouted through his megaphone, 'that certain generals, including those in the most responsible positions of power in our armed forces, are now plotting a military coup. . . . This is not scaremongering, comrades. I have information that the military leadership will no longer tolerate the advance of perestroika, and that it intends to act. . . .'

It was the first time I had heard any public figure speak openly about the dangers of a coup in the Soviet Union; and like most people at the time, I took Urashchev's rhetoric with a pinch of salt. I was, however, interested enough in what he was saying to seek him out at the end of the meeting and to inquire about his sources of information on the way senior generals were thinking. He replied that his organization had collated reports from middle ranking officers throughout the Soviet army, many of whom shared the liberal political views that he and his comrades supported. While a coup may not happen in the next few weeks or months, Shchit had established that certain officers – many of high rank – had been canvassing the opinion of others whom they were inviting to participate in a future conspiracy.

Urashchev continued to warn of the dangers of a coup over the next two and a half years, and other, more established political voices were joined to his, as the threat from a disgruntled army establishment steadily grew.

Even in 1989 there were substantial reasons for believing that the military leadership felt a growing dislike for Gorbachov and his reforms. First there was the natural ideological antipathy to reform felt by an army which had for seventy years been fed on the political values of Communist infallibility. Military doctrine had always targeted the capitalist West as the ultimate enemy; the army's proudest moments were the battles fought for the defence of Stalinism during the Second World War, and too many comrades had been lost in that campaign for the old men at the top of the Soviet military tree to dishonour their memory. For the ordinary soldiers, there had been decades of Communist indoctrination through the all-pervasive system of political officers. Attached to each regiment and charged with maintaining ideological purity among the troops, they were Communism's guarantee of loyalty and like-thinking from an army which the party regarded as its tool, and in which all officers had to be card carrying members of the CPSU. (When a public debate erupted over the issue, with many voices calling for the system of political commissars to be ended, the hardliners won; under intense pressure from military conservatives, Gorbachov publicly declared his opposition to 'depoliticizing' the armed forces in a speech to the Russian Communist Party Congress in June 1990.)

But quite aside from political differences with the Gorbachov regime, the army was also smarting from the slights it believed it had received from the new men in the Kremlin. The final decision to withdraw from Afghanistan in February 1989 was greeted with relief and gratitude by the troops who had fought and suffered there; but one class of Soviet officers saw it as a humiliation and a defeat. These were the men who believed Gorbachov had chickened out and had exposed the army to ridicule by bringing it back from a campaign which should have been pursued to the end. In their eyes, Gorbachov had committed the cardinal error of admitting the fallibility of Communism. The commander of Soviet forces in Afghanistan was Boris Gromov, and two years later he had re-emerged on the Soviet political scene as the country's Deputy Interior Minister, an unflinching hardliner and the right-hand man of Boris Pugo who helped lead the August coup.

Even more damaging for army morale than the retreat from Afghanistan was the retreat from eastern Europe in 1989 and 1990. For forty-five years Soviet military strategy had been based on the need for a buffer zone of subjugated states between the USSR and its potential enemies in the capitalist West. The Red Army's courage in World War Two had won this strategic asset for the country, and now – said the military conservatives – Gorbachov was giving it away. The withdrawal of hundreds of thousands of Soviet troops from the former Communist satellite states was a difficult pill for the army to swallow. It meant a loss of pride; but it also entailed considerable physical hardship. Many soldiers had looked on their tours of duty in Hungary or Czechoslovakia as a reward, a rare opportunity to live in countries where the standard of living was higher and opportunities for professional advancement were more easily available. When the troops began to come home, they faced an appalling situation. Because such a large proportion of its standing army had for four decades been based outside the country, the Soviet Union simply had no place to put them. There were no barracks and no flats for the soldiers; no schools for their children, and no food for their families. Many regiments were consigned to living in tents, with no prospect of any improvement for years ahead. Others were demobbed on the spot and left to fend for themselves in a society where unemployment was already reaching dangerous levels.

The resentment of men who had served their country well and were now being cast aside by the leaders in the Kremlin welled up and eventually spilled over. In the early summer of 1991 I spoke to Poland's Deputy Defence Minister in Warsaw, and he talked about the increasing resistance he had met among Soviet military leaders to continue with the pull-out from eastern Europe. They were, he said, becoming more inflexible about the withdrawal of troops from Poland and about the transit of Soviet troops from the former GDR across Polish territory. Some of the pronouncements by Soviet military officers were, he said, proof that imperial thinking in the Soviet forces was not dead.

The Solidarity leader and politician Adam Michnik went even further, suggesting that the decision to withdraw from eastern

Europe had driven the Soviet military into a fury. He said that since the order to retreat had been received, the head of Soviet forces in Poland, General Dubinin, had begun to address Poles like the commander of an occupying army. He characterized some highly placed Soviet officers as having 'an adventurist attitude which is dangerous for the whole world. If Russia doesn't get rid of these elements, Gorby's head might be the price to pay, the end of Russian democracy. It will be civil war all over again. There will be an ocean of blood, hatred and unhappiness.'

Michnik's remarks were made in June, just two months before the coup. But even within the Soviet Union, indications of the growing discontent of the armed forces over the retreat from eastern Europe had surfaced much earlier. Hardline officers like Colonel Albert Makashov, Commander of the Urals Military District, had spoken out vituperatively about the politicians who had made the decision to withdraw. In a speech at the Congress of Deputies, he accused Eduard Shevardnadze of treason and of 'losing' the former satellites in eastern Europe. An article in the newspaper *Sovietskaya Rossiya*, as always the voice of the hardliners, said that the results of Shevardnadze's policies had had the same effect as if the Soviet Union had fought and lost a Third World War.

The issue of Eastern Europe had helped to focus the army's discontent, and in the months before the attempted coup there were suggestions from some quarters that military commanders were deliberately trying to slow down the withdrawal from Poland and from the former GDR, with the ultimate aim of holding on long enough for a new, more patriotic leadership to come to power in the Kremlin and overturn the decision to pull out. If the possibility of reversing history in such a way was being seriously discussed by men close to the eventual leaders of the August coup, it is disturbing to think what dangerous initiatives might have followed if the coup had succeeded.

Also contributing to the military's discontent was the perception that Gorbachov and Shevardnadze had betrayed their country in their dealings with the United States and NATO. After years of expanding the might of the Soviet military, Gorbachov's arms reduction agreements were now bringing cut-backs and redundancies. The fact that Moscow, in order to achieve an overall balance, had accepted more substantial reductions in several areas of weaponry than Washington was seized on by the hardliners as demonstrating that Gorbachov did not have the interests of his nation (or, more to the point, his military) at heart. There were suggestions that the USSR was being stripped of its ability to defend itself by Gorbachov's irresponsible policies and there was also a widespread feeling in some military circles that the army's pride and prestige were being trampled on.

The military commanders had – like their American counterparts – become used to ever expanding budgets, new projects and ever higher technology. For decades, the military sector had been nurtured and pampered, and given priority over the civilian economy in the race for the USSR to remain a military, if not an industrial, superpower. And while this had had disastrous effects for consumers and workers, it had turned the army into a privileged class apart. When Gorbachov suddenly began talking of cutting military budgets in order to boost spending on civilian projects, and when he made this possible by reducing or abolishing whole ranges of nuclear and conventional weapons, the army's reaction was one of horror. Arms deals with the US also meant cuts in personnel, and what had once been a guaranteed job for life for career soldiers suddenly became filled with uncertainty.

At the end of 1990 the military's anger was vented in a deliberate campaign of sabotage directed against a key treaty reducing conventional forces in Europe. The CFE accord had been signed amidst great celebrations in Paris in November. It was part of a series of multinational agreements which were widely heralded as putting the seal on a 'new world order' of peace and cooperation. The world community had given Gorbachov and Shevardnadze much of the credit for the progress that had been made, but hardline opinion back at home was less than satisfied.

In November 1990 in an off-the-record conversation in his office in the Kremlin, I had talked to Marshal Sergei Akhromeyev. He had earlier quit his post as Chief of Staff on the same day Gorbachov announced the unilateral withdrawal of 500,000 men from eastern Europe, but he had agreed to stay on as chief military adviser to the Soviet President. He told me that he and others like him had felt the cuts were unfairly biased in favour of the Americans, and that many officers believed the Soviet leadership had been weak in not demanding better terms. The CFE arranged for the withdrawal of thousands of troops and the scrapping of large numbers of conventional weapons, including hundreds of battle tanks – which for many in the Soviet military establishment was the last straw. Their response was to look for loopholes in the treaty, and they quickly found one. The CFE accord specifically covered forces on European soil, so the generals decided they would simply move all their best tanks east of the Urals and into the Asian part of the Soviet Union. They would thus be saved from destruction under the treaty, and the weak-kneed liberals in the Kremlin would be taught a lesson.

Eduard Shevardnadze found out about the treachery of his armed forces in the most humiliating way: unenlightened by his own experts, he was eventually presented with irrefutable evidence by the Americans while on a visit to Washington. When I spoke to Shevardnadze three months later, he was still bitter about the army's deceit over the CFE, and he told me that the challenge to his authority by the military hardliners had been a factor in his decision to resign. He mentioned another, earlier, example of the growing defiance of the armed forces. In late 1990, at the height of preparations for the impending Gulf War, Shevardnadze had told the United Nations in New York that if it came to a fight, Moscow would send troops to take part in a UN contingent in the region. But when he returned to Moscow, he found the generals again in revolt against him. They made it plain that for them, the prospect of Soviet soldiers fighting alongside the old enemy America was simply unacceptable; Iraq had previously been an ally of the USSR and some in the military leadership actually wanted to fight with Saddam Hussein, not against him. Shevardnadze was forced to back down, but the incident clearly rankled with him, and he alluded to it (and to the CFE episode) in his resignation speech: 'Things went as far as personal insults,' he said. 'I had to endure that too. Comrades, a campaign of persecution is taking place.' He said no one had come to his defence, and 'boys in colonel's uniforms' had made his position untenable. The warning in Shevardnadze's speech of 'impending dictatorship' was the clearest and most telling warning yet that a coup was in the air.

By this stage, the military hardliners had grown in confidence to the point where they were openly challenging the legally constituted political leadership. Shevardnadze's 'boys in colonels' uniforms' remark was an unmistakable reference to the men who ran Soyuz, the hardline pro-Union group in the parliament. Their most outspoken leader, Colonel Viktor Alksnis, had been upping the stakes in the political confrontation with some increasingly inflammatory remarks. At the 28th Congress of the Communist party, in the summer of 1990, he had openly floated the possibility of a military coup, pretending to deny that a revolt was on the cards, but in fact coming close to threatening one. 'When there is talk of a coup', boomed Alksnis, 'I say: No! We would never go against the people. But I have to tell you that we are now close to the end of our patience. . . .'

At the same Congress, military hardliners had launched a concerted attack on prominent liberals in the Communist party leadership, eventually forcing many of them to resign from the Politburo and the Central Committee. The main target of their anger was Aleksandr Yakovlev, the man credited as the founder of glasnost. Like Eduard Shevardnadze, Yakovlev had supported measures in domestic and foreign policy which the army regarded as harmful to its own interests, and the Congress was their opportunity to hit back. Speech after speech from uniformed delegates attacked Yakovlev, many of them imbued with the age-old rhetoric of Great Russian chauvinism and anti-Semitism (Yakovlev was Jewish).

Eventually, Yakovlev came to the platform to defend himself in an emotional address in which he made it clear that in attacking him and the other liberals, the hardliners were seeking more than just changes in the party leadership – they were seeking the overthrow of perestroika, and they were relying on the threat of military might to do so. From his pocket, he pulled a copy of a leaflet which had been circulated among army delegates at the Congress and which openly called for a coup. 'The leaflet attacks me and my colleagues', Yakovlev told the hall. 'It says, "we need a new Hitler, not Gorbachov." It says, "a military coup is urgently needed." It says, "there is plenty of room in Siberia for the people who gave us this botched perestroika. . . ." Comrades, this is an orchestrated assault!'

There was a some surprise that Gorbachov seemed to offer no resistance to the hardliners' demands, even though he himself was under attack and talk of a coup by the military was being openly bandied about. The reason was that Gorbachov had in fact stood up to the army two months earlier and had, it seemed, lost the battle. On Victory Day, 9 May 1990, the annual parade and holiday which honour the armed forces, Gorbachov had used his speech to the troops from atop Lenin's mausoleum to issue a warning. The army, he said, would have to follow the path of the rest of Soviet society and submit itself to radical changes. The military could not ignore the transformations which had taken place on the domestic and international stages and would have to adapt itself to them. 'We are', said Gorbachov, 'elaborating a plan of perestroika for the armed forces.'

At his 19 August news conference formally announcing his seizure of power, Gennady Yanayev claims Gorbachov has resigned for health reasons. Gorbachov later remarked on Yanayev's trembling fingers and asked, 'who was really sick?' (© Associated Press)

Anatoly Lukyanov, the Chairman of the Soviet Parliament, was the secret mastermind of the coup. He was not arrested until days later, when his role in the conspiracy was revealed. (© Associated Press)

Defence Minister Dimitri Yazov (*above, left*), KGB Chairman Vladimir Kryuchov (*above, right*), Interior Minister Boris Pugo (*right*) and Prime Minister Valentin Pavlov (*below, right*) were Yanayev's co-conspirators in the August plot. They had already attempted to overthrow Gorbachov two months earlier, but he had failed to heed the warning and had not acted to remove them. (© Associated Press)

On 19 August, popular resistance to the tanks and troops began immediately. The pre-revolutionary Russian flag became a potent symbol of defiance. (© Associated Press)

When tanks were sent to besiege the Russian parliament where Boris Yeltsin had taken refuge, they were met with boos and jeers from demonstrators on the parliament steps. (© Associated Press)

Anti-coup demonstrators, fearing an all-out military assault on the Russian parliament, spent three days and nights manning makeshift barricades: they were defending Boris Yeltsin and democracy. (A. Nogues/Sygma)

Violence flared during the night of Tuesday, 20 August, when tanks tried to smash through lines of buses used as barricades by pro-democracy demonstrators. (© Associated Press)

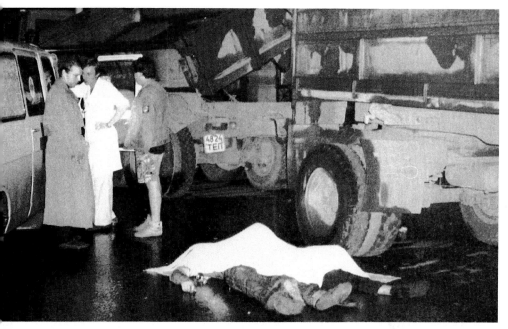

The fiercest fighting was on the Inner Ring Road close to the Russian parliament. Three young men were killed by the tanks. (© Associated Press)

The commanders of the tank column which killed the three protesters were surrounded and forced to surrender to the crowds. (© Associated Press)

The tanks began to withdraw from Moscow on the afternoon of Wednesday, 21 August: the Russian people had defeated the coup. (© Associated Press)

22 August. Mikhail Gorbachov flies back to Moscow after three days of captivity in the Crimea. He said he had returned to 'a different world'. (© Associated Press)

Boris Yeltsin was quick to show Gorbachov who was the new master of the country: he humiliated the Soviet president at a session of the Russian parliament, forcing Gorbachov to read out a list of his own ministers who had taken part in the coup. (© Gamma, photo by Shone)

The funeral of the three victims of the tanks brought thousands on to the streets. It was a moment of emotional and spiritual rebirth for Russia. (© Associated Press)

Boris Yeltsin was the ultimate beneficiary of the coup. His stand in defence of democracy won him public adulation and overwhelming political power. (© Gamma, photo by Georges Merillon)

It was a direct challenge to the army command, and Dmitri Yazov made an immediate riposte in his speech. 'Yes,' said Yazov, 'reforms will continue . . . but we must not forget that our country is still facing a military threat, and our armed forces must be maintained in a state of readiness with the capacity to defend our homeland.' The tension between the Marshal and the President was obvious.

It surfaced again later in the year in a televized meeting of all the armed forces' top commanders, where Gorbachov was invited to attend and hear the grievances of the military establishment. The only civilian among a sea of uniforms, Gorbachov vainly tried to defend himself as millions watched on TV. Yazov was the chief inquisitor, throwing questions about material problems facing soldiers, such as the lack of accommodation and reduced prospects for promotion. The arguments spread into a wider policy debate about the question of funding for the army, the lack of necessary facilities and the suggestion that budget cuts were leaving the country unprepared for any foreign military aggression. There was talk of the loss of honour and dignity of the armed forces. Yazov made it clear that many generals resented Gorbachov's policies which had ended the army's role abroad and reduced its prestige at home; and Gorbachov, surrounded by their massed ranks, looked uncomfortable and browbeaten. Afterwards, the liberal editor of *Ogonyok* magazine, Vitaly Korotich, commented, 'Now at least Gorbachov knows who his enemies are. . . .'

The result of the arguments in May, and the behind the scenes negotiations which presumably followed, was that Gorbachov was henceforth much less willing to seek confrontation with his military commanders. In light of future events, the Victory Day polemics may have been an important turning point.

To many people Gorbachov was beginning to seem irretrievably weak. He was widely accused of putting the gains of perestroika at risk by not taking a firmer line with the army. But the President was struggling to cope with very real pressures. Already in February 1990 the army had staged a threatening show of strength in Moscow during the mass demonstration called by the liberals to demand the abolition of Article 6 of the Constitution, which guaranteed Communism's leading political role in society. As previously mentioned, Gorbachov had given his blessing to the demonstration, and was making no secret of his intention to support the ending of the Communist monopoly in the Central Committee. To the deeply pro-Communist elements in the army, this was an open provocation.

Days before the rally, reports began to circulate that the military was planning to break up the demonstration and teach the radicals a lesson they would never forget. Some sort of putsch was widely rumoured and there were unprecedented official warnings on national television and radio, telling people to stay away from the rally because of the possibility of violence. Prime Minister Nikolai Ryzhkov made a personal appeal for restraint and the maintenance of order at the demonstration. On Sunday, 4 February, we all gathered outside Gorky Park in an atmosphere of foreboding, and as the hundreds of thousands of demonstrators followed the well-trodden path from the Park, around the ring-road and down Gorky Street to Manezhnaya Square, there was a large and obvious presence of troops and police. But there was no attempt to stop the march and in the event it passed off peacefully. We later heard that army units had been assembled in a Moscow suburb, but did not receive the order to move into the city centre.

There was no way of checking these reports, nor the suggestions that an army delegation had been sent to the Kremlin to present Gorbachov with a list of demands, threatening mayhem if he did not comply. Gorbachov's officials later denied that he had received any army representatives that day, or that he had caved in to their demands. An increased toughness in Soviet attitudes at East-West arms reduction talks in the weeks which followed the demonstration was cited as proof that a deal had been struck with the military, but again this was purely circumstantial evidence. What was certain, though, was that the atmosphere of public uncertainty in the Soviet Union had reached the point where rumours of an impending coup could no longer be dismissed, and where the potential role of the army had become a crucial element in the political equation.

In September 1990 a build-up of military manoeuvres around Moscow sparked another round of speculation. Boris Yeltsin reported to the Russian parliament that he was concerned about the army's intentions, and on 28 September Gavriil Popov, the Mayor of Moscow, called a news conference to express his alarm. 'Our information,' he said, 'is that a group of extremists is preparing to take action on October 6th or 7th, on the understanding that conservative forces will find in these actions reasons to impose a state of emergency.'

When radicals in the Supreme Soviet tried to bring the same 'information' to the attention of Gorbachov, he flew into a rage and began to attack the deputies who had spoken out. 'Let them bring me proof!' he shouted. 'They must bring concrete names and firm evidence and report it to me here!' His outburst implied that he believed the deputies were talking nonsense, but his anger may have reflected his fear that a coup was no longer such a far-fetched possibility. There was no proof that a putsch was being planned, but the willingness of the people to believe and repeat the rumours both reflected and increased the tension which was gripping society.

When Boris Yeltsin's car was accidentally rammed by a passing Lada on Gorky Street, the Moscow grapevine immediately circulated the news that this had been an assassination attempt in preparation for a military takeover. In any event, Gorbachov considered the coup-mania to be sufficiently worrying to call Dmitri Yazov to the Supreme Soviet to deny publicly all the rumours that were circulating. Yeltsin's accident, said Yazov, was merely an unfortunate incident, and not the work of sinister forces. The troops around the city, he continued, were not preparing to march on Moscow, but were simply being assembled to help harvest the potato crop; the military had no designs on power. In the end, nothing untoward happened on 6 or 7 October.

If the rumblings of the military were growing to a roar by the end of 1990, they were given an additional – perhaps decisive boost – by a sudden turn for the worse in the already critical state of the Soviet economy. In the early days of October, bread disappeared from the shops of Moscow for the first time in forty-five years. It was impossible to find a loaf anywhere in the city: I toured dozens of bread shops, and all had the same story – no deliveries, so no bread. There had, of course, been many shortages of many different items at times in the past, but bread was special. It was central to Russian eating habits – and bakeries often displayed the slogan, *Khleb golova vsemu* (Bread is the source of all good things) – and its disappearance had a deep psychological effect. In many areas queues and panic buying spilled over into arguments, then fights, until widespread public unrest became a genuine threat.

For the week or so that the shortage persisted, all sorts of theories circulated about the reasons behind it, and many liberals suggested the cause was deliberate sabotage. Ever since a radical city council had been elected in Moscow, there had been sporadic attempts to undermine their authority. Country areas surrounding the capital, which were still governed by old-style Communists, had repeatedly refused to send the city the food supplies it had regularly received in the past. This had caused the periodic disappearance of staple items from the shops (milk vanished at one stage; later it was eggs, and then meat), and the cause was always the same: political mischief-making by enemies of the reformist liberals. The October bread crisis, though, caused deep consternation. The liberals accused the KGB and the hardliners of deliberately disrupting the supply and distribution system, and older people recalled with anxiety that the same thing had happened just before the ousting of Nikita Khrushchev in 1964: food was withheld from the shops to discredit Khrushchev and it returned in abundance once the new regime had been installed.

The shortages in 1990 played into the hands of the hardliners and the army: they could point to clear evidence that perestroika was not working and use it to fuel their demands for violent change. But while individual disruptions in the food supply may well have been the result of deliberate sabotage, it was ultimately the failure of Gorbachov himself to make any impression on the country's economic decline which had created the discontent the hardliners were now seeking to exploit.

Gorbachov had remained an effective manipulator of the political levers of power, but the economy was his Achilles' heel. Instead of the improvements he had promised in living standards, his leadership had seen a dramatic decline in almost every economic indicator. It was this more than anything which turned public opinion against him and which provided fertile ground for those who plotted to overthrow him. For the latter half of 1990 and the first months of 1991, Soviet economic policy was paralysed, and much of the blame must go to Gorbachov himself. A long-drawn-out argument over the pace of economic change was never effectively resolved because of his indecision.

In August 1990 Gorbachov had indicated that he would give his support to a radical plan, the so-called Shatalin-Yavlinsky 500 programme, drawn up by two liberal economists close to Boris Yeltsin, which aimed to open up the old central command economy to market forces and the chill wind of free enterprise and competition. Its authors recognized that the rapid transition to a Western-style market economy would involve austerity measures, higher prices and unemployment; but they argued that the end result of a healthy economic system would be worth the cost. Gorbachov was initially highly enthusiastic and agreed with Boris Yeltsin to cooperate on the plan's introduction in Russia and across the

Union. But soon afterwards his long-serving Prime Minister Nikolai Ryzhkov, stressed to him the social costs of such a rapid economic transformation. Clearly frightened by tales of massive job losses, inflation and public unrest, the President promised to rethink his decision, and he also asked Ryzhkov to produce his own plan for a slower, more cautious transition to a market system. This Ryzkov did, in association with his own economic guru Leonid Abalkin, whereupon Gorbachov agreed to go along with his version.

But again Gorbachov's indecision got the better of him, and his public hesitations involved the Supreme Soviet in convoluted votes and amendments for several days. Neither of the authors of the two plans could pin the President down. Nikolai Ryzhkov told me later that he was exasperated with Gorbachov's unreliability, and he pointed out the potential dangers of his inconsistency. The lack of a coordinated economic policy, said Ryzhkov, could lead to public discontent and play into the hands of those who wanted to impose the 'firm hand' of dictatorship. 'Gorbachov is again acting in an ill-considered way,' he said, looking momentarily surprised by his own outspokenness. 'I am not afraid to say that. . . . I think it is dangerous, simply dangerous. There might come a time when the pressure builds up and society could explode.' This, of course, is precisely what the hardliners were counting on.

In the end, Gorbachov showed his penchant for trying to reconcile the irreconcilable and ordered that the two plans 'should be merged'. Yavlinsky said it was like trying to mate a hedgehog with a snake, and the result (known laughably as the Gorbachov plan) was a mishmash of economic nonsequiturs. Not surprisingly, it stood little chance of being implemented despite parliamentary votes to put it into practice. Moreover, when Gorbachov pulled out of his cooperation accord with the Russian leadership, Boris Yeltsin announced that his republic would go ahead alone with the 500 day programme. It was fighting talk, but in the end it was to no avail: without the backing of the Soviet authorities, Russia could have no hope of effecting such far-reaching economic reforms on its own, and the plan was eventually abandoned.

While Gorbachov fiddled, Moscow was beginning to smoulder. Economic tinkering without an overall strategy was sparking public discontent. Attempts to remove state subsidies and raise prices in the shops were hastily ended after widespread public anger ran through the city and panic buying emptied what little there was left in the shops. The Alice in Wonderland economics of Valentin Pavlov, who replaced Ryzhkov as Prime Minister in January 1991, caused even greater alarm when he cancelled without notice all 50- and 100- rouble denomination bank-notes. Pavlov said the aim was to destroy the black market, whose mafia godfathers were reputed to keep their ill-gotten gains in large denominations. In practice, the villains managed to salvage their profits, and it was ordinary folk whose savings were wiped out when they found the notes they had been holding were now worthless. Pavlov went even further with his wild accusations that the West was planning an 'economic coup' to flood the USSR with surplus roubles and cause the destruction of the Soviet currency. In fact, the currency was almost worthless anyway, there was no Western plot, and Pavlov seems to have been using the age-old scapegoat strategy, which for Soviet leaders meant stirring up anti-Western hysteria and deflecting blame onto the capitalists. His later role as one of the leaders of the August coup may even suggest that his accusations against the West could have had an ulterior motive. While Pavlov was expressing anti-Westernism, the Soviet public was witnessing Gorbachov himself embarking on a campaign to involve the capitalist countries in rescuing the Soviet economy. His reasoning was that the West wanted the USSR to reform its economy, which would be in the West's own interests, so it should help out, preferably with large amounts of cash. Already in the winter months of 1990–91 the Kremlin had been actively encouraging reports that famine was once again stalking the Soviet Union and that widespread malnutrition was inevitable unless the West sent food aid. The facts were rather less dramatic: although there were shortages of some foods, no one was dying, and the appeals for Western aid had the aura of a propaganda tool. The West – in particular, the old enemy Germany – did send planeloads of food, addressed to children's homes and hospitals, only for it to be syphoned off by the omnipresent Soviet mafia, with much of it ending up on the black market.

The spectacle of the Soviet Union going on bended knee to the West – and, worst of all to the Germans, whom the Red Army was supposed to have defeated in 1945 – was too much for the hardliners. They accused Gorbachov of undermining Soviet pride and humbling the USSR before the country which had produced the curse of Nazism.

Even worse was to come, as Gorbachov began to formulate his appeal for extended Western participation in his economic reforms.

When he received an invitation – long angled for – to the summit of the world's seven leading industrialized nations in London in July, he seized his opportunity. Using a mixture of bribery and blackmail, he called on the West to invest heavily in the Soviet Union's future – he himself mentioned the figure of 100 billion dollars – offering in return a clear, irrevocable commitment to the adoption of a market economy. The implications were that the West would be rewarded for its generosity by seeing the USSR develop into a good member of the capitalist world order. The veiled threat, formulated overtly in London by Gorbachov's adviser, Yevgeny Primakov, was that failure to bale out the Soviet economy could not only undermine Gorbachov's position, but leave him vulnerable to a conservative attempt to remove him from power. That, ran the Soviet argument, could trigger an economic and political disintegration of the country which would send dangerous shock waves in the West's own direction, in the form of millions of refugees and a collapse of the European trade and economic equilibrium.

In the event, Gorbachov's bluff was called. Under the influence of the hard-nosed Americans, British and Japanese, the G7 refused to put any cash on the table, offering instead technical assistance, advice and kind words – a parsimonious short-sightedness which later sparked anxious recriminations among Western leaders: if we had baled Gorbachov out, ran the argument, maybe the opposition to him would have been defused and the danger of a coup averted. Gorbachov's conservative critics had been outspoken in condemning his attendance at G7, and the outcome – taken together with his acceptance of German food aid – helped crystallize a hardline complaint that Gorbachov was selling out to the West without gaining any tangible reward.

There is little doubt that by the time of the August putsch Gorbachov was very unpopular in the Soviet Union, and many people welcomed the coup because they hoped it would at least provide some hope of material improvement. While the Gorbachov years had brought freedom of thought and intellectual expression, this had satisfied only the intelligentsia and freedom to complain had bred demands for more substantial changes. Among the ordinary people, it meant pressure for economic improvements, and these did not materialize. Previous Soviet regimes which presided over living conditions bordering on destitution had not felt the wrath of the people, because the people had expected little else. Gorbachov, though, had created expectations which were not met. Taken together with the dissent over Gorbachov's approaches to the capitalist countries, the atmosphere was ripe for hardline agitation.

Under such circumstances, the August plotters were led to believe they could win over the majority of the people to support their overtly anti-Gorbachov campaign. What the putschists failed to understand was that only half the Soviet people disliked their president for being too radical, too reformist and too Westward-looking. The other half, which eventually confounded the coup leaders' plans, disliked Gorbachov for not being radical enough; and when they gained the upper hand, they pressed successfully for more – not less – radical reform, securing the victory not of the hardline Communists but of the Yeltsinite liberals.

There was, however, one final dress rehearsal before the August coup could take place: the January putsch in Lithuania and Latvia. It was completely in character for the hardliners in the military to choose the Baltic states for their first concerted attempt at seizing power, because the main target for their anger had by then become the disintegration of the USSR and the concessions Gorbachov was preparing to offer the separatist republics in his new Union Treaty.

The root of the problem went back to Gorbachov's first years in power, when his policy of glasnost quickly unleashed long-pent-up tensions among the Soviet Union's one hundred or more ethnic groups. Local rivalries, ethnic hatreds, desires for revenge, quarrels over land rights and – most potent of all – the thirst for independence were all given expression for the first time in many decades. Gorbachov had decided to strive for social justice at the expense of imposed order, and this had allowed long frustrated grievances to surface, sometimes with violent consequences.

The hardliners were quick to seize on the disorder and violence which had crept into Soviet society as the result of Gorbachov's policies, and they used the spectre of ethnic divisions very effectively to argue that the time had come for a return to the old system of firm rule. With more and more republics pressing to leave the Union, army hardliners were becoming increasingly united behind the banner of direct action – violent if necessary – to stop the dismemberment of the fatherland. At a stormy meeting with Gorbachov in the Kremlin on 13 November 1990, more than a thousand officers from the armed forces harangued the President and pressed him to take action. Typical were the comments of Major Andrei Sokorchuk who had been stationed in the western Ukraine and had seen the effects of nationalist sentiment there: 'Anti-socialist, separatist forces have taken over the local councils . . .' he complained. 'The situation needs immediate, resolute action. Delay will be fatal.' And Sokorchuk called on Gorbachov to take such action at once: 'When is all this going to stop? When is the national leadership going to defend us and our honour?'

Other army leaders were not prepared to wait for the President. At the same time as the Kremlin confrontation, Marshal Sergei Akhromeyev wrote in the army newspaper *Krasnaya Zvezda* (Red Banner) that the armed forces were ready to act 'to protect the unity of our homeland and to preserve the constitutional order. The time has come to defend our state with courage and resolution.' Gorbachov seemed to have taken the military's message to heart. In a speech to the Supreme Soviet in December, he stated his own strong support for the preservation of the Union, reversing previous suggestions he had made about letting rebellious republics leave. 'I will not let our great, multinational country fall apart,' he told the parliament, '.. any attempt to separate peoples who have lived side by side for centuries could turn into a blood bath . . .'

This was at the height of Gorbachov's swing to the conservatives, and he softened his position considerably when he moved back to the liberals in the Spring of 1991. But his tough stance on the question of Soviet unity at that time seemed to indicate that he had accepted, in part at least, the military's view that the creeping indiscipline and chaos in society must be brought under control. His indication of support seems, in turn, to have played a role in reassuring the generals that they would not meet any concerted opposition to their plans for a putsch in the Baltics.

Gorbachov's attitude to the separatist Baltic republics had fluctuated since Lithuania first declared its independence on 11 March 1990. An initial attempt to brow-beat the Balts into submission had involved him in threats, presidential decrees and a lengthy economic blockade which left the Lithuanians without petrol for their cars, heating for their homes or – for part of the time – food for their tables. In the face of determined resistance from the Lithuanian people, Gorbachov had softened his position. A farcical 'suspension' of the republic's independence declaration had won an end to the blockade and the offer of talks with a central government commission led by Prime Minister Nikolai Ryzhkov. Those negotiations had dragged on for months with no perceptible progress and were brought to an abrupt end when Gorbachov made the hardliners in the autumn of 1990. The unholy alliance of the president and the generals came to fruition in January, in the Baltic massacres which Gorbachov later claimed he did not order, but which nonetheless happened with his connivance and were undoubtedly made more likely to happen by his tough public stance on the issue.

With the world's attention distracted by the impending war in the Gulf, the Soviet Defence Ministry announced at the beginning of January that it was sending thousands of paratroopers to republics which had active separatist movements. The reason given was the need to enforce the spring draft of conscripts to the army; but there was a widely felt suspicion that this was, at last, the translation into action of all the threatening words the military strong-men had been uttering for so many months. The first indications that this was the case came with the occupation by Soviet troops of a print-works in the Latvian capital, Riga, which had been used to publish nationalist newspapers. The following day, Soviet television showed a documentary accusing the Baltic separatists of being neo-fascists who fought with the Nazis during the war, and accusing Western intelligence services of involvement in the stirring of nationalist unrest. The rhetoric was another throw back to the cold war years, and all the signs of impending military repression were beginning to appear.

In the Soviet parliament, liberal deputies called for the withdrawal of the paratroopers, but were met with contempt. The 'black colonel' Viktor Alksnis, himself half-Latvian, said, 'This confrontation was started by the Baltics, not by Moscow. So I believe it is now necessary to introduce martial law there.' Anatoly Lukyanov, a future plotter himself, fed the parliament barefaced lies in a voice of utter complacency: 'The view that there has been some kind of swing to the right, or a dangerous coalition of conservative forces willing to introduce dictatorship, simply does not correspond to the facts.'

Clashes broke out between nationalist demonstrators and pro-Moscow groups outside the Lithuanian parliament. After the mainly Russian Unionists tried to storm it, President Vytautas Landsbergis barricaded himself and his government inside and appealed for Lithuanians to come and defend the building, just as Boris Yeltsin was to do seven months later. Landsbergis spoke of a decisive historical moment which was about to determine the whole future of reform in the Soviet Union.

In Moscow, Yeltsin condemned the decision to send troops to the Baltics and said violence would breed greater violence. But Gorbachov appeared on Soviet television with a threat of even tougher measures to come: 'Urgent measures must be adopted . . . the people are demanding the restoration of constitutional order . . . they are demanding the imposition of presidential rule.' Hours later, the troops seized more buildings in the Lithuanian capital. Two days later they stormed the Vilnius television station, killing thirteen unarmed civilians who had been defending the building. Gorbachov claimed that he had not given the orders and called for a negotiated political solution; but Boris Yeltsin had little doubt where the blame must lie, and he said so on national television: 'I warned in 1987 that Gorbachov lusted after power. Now he has a dictatorship with a pretty name, "Presidential Rule". . . . I call for his immediate resignation'.

Only a week after receiving the Nobel Peace Prize, Gorbachov had presided over the bloody repression of peaceful civilians and his credibility as a liberal reformer was in tatters. On the eve of the massacre he had publicly promised there would be no military action, a promise which was made to seem either a cynical piece of deceit, or – more likely – an indication that his hardline military accomplices had taken things into their own hands.

Just days later it was Latvia's turn. The Vilnius killings had been a chilling forewarning to the Latvians, and they quickly prepared makeshift defences on the streets of Riga. Barricades of lorries and buses were supplemented with huge concrete blocks, barring the way to the Latvian parliament, and thousands of civilian volunteers spent days and nights on the streets, braving sub-zero temperatures to try to defend their nation's freedom. Here too, though, Moscow's troops left their mark with wanton violence. After days of vicious attacks on nationalist barricades, the troops staged a concerted assault on the Latvian Council of Ministers building, again leaving a trail of death and destruction. Again Gorbachov denied responsibility, but again it was his decision not to oppose the hardliners and the military which allowed the killings to happen.

One personal memory of those Baltic nights makes it hard for me to give Gorbachov any benefit of the doubt over the January killings. In the nightmarish atmosphere of Riga under siege, my guides and companions had been a team of young film-makers from Lithuania: they had recorded and survived the massacre at the Vilnius TV tower and now they had come to film the fate of their Latvian comrades.

I said goodnight to them outside a barricaded church and never saw them again: they were shot dead by Moscow's soldiers, shot deliberately in the back because they were filming the fighting at the Council of Ministers building.

The apportioning of blame for the Baltic killings will inevitably centre on the role of Gorbachov. Unlike during the days of the August coup, he was in the Kremlin, supposedly bearing ultimate responsibility for the running of the country. Previous experience over the killing of civilians by troops in the Georgian capital of Tbilisi in April 1989 suggests that any independent investigation, were it to be held, would meet concerted efforts to hinder its inquiries. Anatoly Sobchak, who led the parliamentary scrutiny of the Tbilisi events, told me that even in that instance (when Gorbachov was out of the country and consequently absolved of any involvement in ordering the troops to attack) there was considerable resistance to his inquiries, and even to publishing his report.

The Baltic events are further complicated by the elaborate facade of disclaimed responsibility which the conspirators built up around themselves. Gorbachov said he was asleep at the time of the attacks and found out about them only when he awoke the following morning; the military leadership in Moscow announced that it had not ordered the killings; and the army commanders on the ground said they had received instructions from the self-styled National Salvation Committees which had sprung up in Latvia and Lithuania, claiming that they were taking charge of republics because the nationalist governments had forfeited the trust of the people. But nearly all the 'members' of the Salvation Committees remained anonymous and there was considerable doubt about whether they were anything other than front organizations for the local hardline, pro-Moscow Communist parties.

So the trail seems to peter out and there is little hope that anyone will ever be brought to justice for the killings. (The official Soviet Prosecutor's report stated cynically that the deaths were the result of actions by the separatists themselves and that Soviet troops had been fired on and attacked.) But the fact remains that the shadowy Salvation Committees had no legal or elected status, no right to claim they were replacing the democratic governments of the republics, and no right to issue orders to Soviet troops to kill Soviet civilians. Some measure of responsibility must therefore lie with those who gave the Salvation Committees enough status to carry out their attempted putsch. Gorbachov is certainly guilty of that: even after the killings, he was still speaking of the Salvation Committees as if they were legally recognized bodies, and saying that the local military commanders were responding to the Committees' requests for 'protection' when they moved in to attack the nationalists. A remark he made to the Supreme Soviet – 'We did not want this to happen' – was the closest he ever came to admitting responsibility.

Yazov and Pugo, the future plotters in August, rationalised and justified the Baltic killings, implicating themselves and their ministries in the massacres. When Yazov appeared before the Supreme Soviet to give the army's explanation for the events in the Baltics, he blamed the whole affair squarely on the separatists, saying they had established bourgeois dictatorships which were challenging Soviet power. Pugo, too, had few regrets, telling a national television audience that the Salvation Committees were legitimate authorities which were protecting the interests of the working class, and that the soldiers had acted in self-defence.

When the paratroops were withdrawn from the Baltics a week later, it was widely assumed that the men in the Kremlin who were behind the Baltic crack-down had had an attack of cold feet or had quarrelled among themselves. Some Gorbachov aides suggested in private conversation that the President had convinced others who were bent on pursuing the campaign that nothing was to be gained by further action. Whatever the truth of that, there was no doubting that the hardliners in the military – with or without Gorbachov's backing - had shown their hand in the Baltics.

It was equally clear that the deep rooted grievances which had prompted them to act in January had not been removed as a result of the putsch, and the fear remained that the same men (Yazov and Pugo remained in power, with no overt challenge to their position) would be more than likely to try again. Gorbachov had done little to impede their actions in the Baltics and did nothing to curb their power in the months to come. The attempted coup in Lithuania and Latvia had served as a warning that no one appears to have heeded, least of all the man who would be the plotters' main target next time they chose to act.

6

The Apotheosis of Boris Yeltsin

The August coup ruined the fortunes of many Soviet politicians, but it set the seal on the career of one. From being a discarded outsider with no political future, Boris Yeltsin returned from obscurity. His role during the August events made him effectively the most powerful man in the Soviet Union. Without his courage and resolve, resistance to the coup would have been fractured, and the plotters' chances of triumphing would have been infinitely greater. He held aloft the banner of liberal reformist values, and his reward was to displace Mikhail Gorbachov as the moral leader of the nation.

But the path which brought Yeltsin to his moment of destiny in the Russian parliament was a complex one. The forming of a political personality capable of resisting the threats of the would-be dictators was based on chance as much as deliberate intent; and in the final analysis, Yeltsin's apotheosis was due in equal part to his personal, reciprocated hatred of Mikhail Gorbachov and to the unprecedented humaneness of the political system Gorbachov had created.

The picture Boris Yeltsin paints of his childhood in his autobiography is of a young man always in conflict with authority. He quarrelled with his teachers, with his peers and with his political mentors. But in all these clashes, it was Yeltsin who was right and the others who were wrong. If Yeltsin lost an argument, it was always because he was being unfairly victimized; and he saved up his rancour at such treatment to effect his revenge at a future stage. The early autobiography is a revealing self-portrait, betraying the character faults which Yeltsin exploited to his advantage in his later political career: an implicit self-belief which easily spilled over into bullying; a patient and ever-smouldering need to right the wrongs (real or imagined) that others had inflicted on him; a desire for personal recognition, even adulation; and an implacable cruelty to his enemies once they had been laid low.

But from the moment Yeltsin shakes your hand in an unrelenting grip which seems destined to shatter your fingers, it is impossible to escape the force and presence of his personality. He is the epitome of the charismatic politician, much more so than Mikhail Gorbachov, who has intellectual presence and a nimble mind but lacks the ever-present, underlying mental threat which Yeltsin exudes – the unvoiced expression in his eyes which says, 'if you disagree with me, I will crush you.' If Gorbachov loses his temper he goes red in the face; if Yeltsin gets angry he directs his rage coldly and deliberately at its target.

But with all that, he is a charming man. He has the burly frame and the battered face of a heavy-weight boxer, but when he smiles it is the face of a mischievous boy. He has all the studied mannerisms of a politician, conscious of the power of body language (Yeltsin keeps his left hand, which was maimed by a hand-grenade he picked up as a young child, out of public view: his gestures are nearly all made with his right hand alone); but at the same time he has retained a spontaneous Russian openness, even naivety, which is his political trump card and has won him the admiration and affection of the man in the street, and the sighs and devotion of nearly every Russian woman.

There is no doubt that Yeltsin has a formidable public personality. He has the rare gift of inspiring unquestioning personal loyalty (or in some cases, implacable hatred); and he can persuade a crowd or a nation that they should follow him to the ends of the earth. But for many years this awesome political machine seemed to be turning in a void. Yeltsin seemed to have no clear idea of a political cause or a social ideal to which his vast potential might be harnessed, a man without personal convictions, seeking for any movement which might employ his talents. Were it not for a series of chance events and the quirks of his personality, it is conceivable that he could have ended up in the camp of the men he eventually came to oppose and defeat.

Like any other aspiring young Russian politician, Yeltsin joined the only political party allowed to exist in his country. With his characteristic drive and desire for recognition, he rose quickly through the Communist hierarchy, becoming party boss in his native Sverdlovsk. The man who was later to become an outspoken liberal, showed a ready willingness at that time to embrace the excesses of old-guard Communism. The energy and enthusiasm which had been seeking an outlet was poured unreservedly into the first cause which was offered to him, and that was the cause of Brezhnevite dogma.

During Yeltsin's drive for the Russian presidency in 1991, when he was campaigning on a radical reformist platform, we dug out some old black and white news-reel footage of his time in Sverdlovsk. It showed him as the local party boss leading May Day parades with all the old-style Communist slogans. In one of his speeches praising the ideals he would later come to abhor, he said of Leonid Brezhnev, the man whose legacy – in the form of the old-guard plotters – he later opposed and defeated: 'The people are deeply grateful for the titanic efforts of the Central Committee of the Communist Party of the Soviet Union, the Politburo, and personally to Leonid Ilyich Brezhnev for his outstanding role in developing and implementing all aspects of our domestic and foreign policy.' It was an undisguised plea for advancement from an ambitious local party leader, a reminder to the central authorities that Boris Yeltsin's talents were being neglected, and that Yeltsin himself was on the verge of feeling slighted.

When the call to Moscow eventually came, though, it was not from the old-guard leadership, but from a new brand of Soviet leader. It was Mikhail Gorbachov who gave Yeltsin his chance to prove himself at the highest level of Soviet politics, appointing him a Secretary of the Central Committee in July 1985; and it was Mikhail Gorbachov who oversaw Yeltsin's rise in the national leadership. In December 1985 he was made Moscow party boss, and in February 1986 a candidate (or non-voting) member of the Politburo.

Yeltsin's enthusiasm had by then been switched from old-guard Brezhnevite Communism to the new ideals of perestroika and glasnost. He was regarded as a Gorbachov protégé and he devoted his energies to promoting his mentor's vision of limited, middle of the road reform. It was at this stage of his career that Yeltsin's personal traits played a crucial part in forming his future political views. In a now famous clash at the Central Committee plenum of October 1987, Yeltsin quarrelled furiously with Gorbachov. The cause of the quarrel, Gorbachov claimed, was Yeltsin's overweening ambition and his complaints that his talents were not being adequately recognized. Yeltsin claimed that Gorbachov had not responded to his ideas for intensifying the perestroika campaign, and the crux of his fateful speech at the October plenum was a personal attack on Gorbachov himself: 'Recently there has been a noticeable increase in what I can only call the adulation of the General Secretary by certain members of the Politburo. . . .this tendency to adulation is absolutely unacceptable. . . .to develop a taste for adulation can lead to a new "cult of personality". This must not be allowed.'

Gorbachov's response was telling: 'Boris Nikolaevich . . . you have reached such a level of vanity and self-regard that you put your ambitions higher than the interests of the party, than the interests of our work . . . at a time when perestroika has reached such a critical stage, I consider this highly irresponsible.'

Complaining that he felt 'out of place' in the Politburo, and that he had not received proper support from his colleagues, Yeltsin asked to be allowed to resign. His speech clearly suggests that he felt slighted by Gorbachov, and by the conservative Yegor Ligachov who still enjoyed considerable influence in the leadership, and much of his future conduct seemed to stem directly from the personality clash at the time of the October plenum. He had written a letter to Gorbachov in which he speaks of 'a discernible change from an attitude of friendly support to one of indifference towards matters concerning Moscow and coldness towards me personally'.

From this time Yeltsin nursed a personal dislike of Gorbachov and a constant desire for revenge. He took delight in the General Secretary's travails and consciously added to them by his own behaviour. The personal enmity seemed to influence his political behaviour too. As Gorbachov began to impose limits on the extent of reform he was prepared to tolerate, Yeltsin became increasingly extreme in his demands for immediate radical change. In many instances it was clear that Gorbachov would not or could not meet Yeltsin's demands, and Yeltsin took obvious satisfaction from exposing his former mentor to liberal criticism and to charges of hampering the reform process.

For three years after the October plenum, Yeltsin played the role of critical opposition to Gorbachov. His attacks were often full of malice and were short on constructive policies. When Gorbachov said it was too early for the Soviet Union to have fully open elections, Yeltsin replied by demanding such elections immediately; when Gorbachov admitted that the transition to a market economy would involve austerity measures, Yeltsin appeared on national television to claim that he could make the transition without affecting people's living standards.

It was this period which earned Yeltsin the reputation of being a political maverick of little substance. His pressure for immediate radical reform was seen as being irresponsible and provocative, while

Gorbachov's moderate, step by step approach was regarded as taking into account the realities of a political situation which would only tolerate a restrained pace of change. Western politicians in particular viewed Yeltsin's policies as largely destructive: Yeltsin knew he could attack Gorbachov and make exorbitant promises about his own capabilities because he was not in power and there was no immediate prospect of him being called on to carry out his claims in practice. (The Bush administration was particularly dismissive of Yeltsin at this stage, describing him privately as 'flaky'.)

The very fact that Yeltsin was allowed to continue his political career after such a public and definitive fall from grace was in itself unprecedented in the Soviet Union. Under Stalin, similar opposition to the General Secretary would have ended in a prison camp or a firing squad. Even under Khrushchev it would have meant banishment from political life and the fate of a 'non person'. But under Gorbachov, the new atmosphere of openness meant that even political opponents might be offered a second chance. In Yeltsin's case, that second chance came directly from Gorbachov himself.

In his autobiography, Yeltsin recounts that on 17 November, less than a month after their acrimonious clash, Gorbachov rang him to offer him the job of Deputy Chairman of the State Construction Committee, with the rank of junior minister. Had Gorbachov merely kept quiet, and had Yeltsin been left to return to Sverdlovsk, he might simply have disappeared from public life. Gorbachov would thus have been spared Yeltsin's constant attacks, the demagogy and the rabble rousing, and much of the pressure from the radical extreme of the ideological spectrum which was to make his political balancing act so difficult in the years ahead. But as with his decision to hold open parliamentary elections at the beginning of 1989, Gorbachov may have looked on Yeltsin as a counterweight to the conservatives in his administration, a controllable liberal force which he could use to balance out the pressure from the hardliners. Whatever his reasoning, Gorbachov clearly miscalculated in allowing Yeltsin the most remarkable political come-back of Soviet history. But he also secured the political survival of the one man who would lead the triumph of democracy during the August coup, defeating the revisionists and allowing Gorbachov himself to return from his imprisonment in the Crimea.

Yeltsin, for whatever reasons, had now thrown in his lot with the extreme wing of liberal activism, and was to be the goad which kept the process of perestroika moving forward by demanding more than the system could offer and waiting for it to catch up. When I talked to him in his office at the State Construction Committee in early 1989, his political fortunes were about to take another leap forward: Yeltsin was then campaigning in the elections to the new Congress of People's Deputies which Gorbachov had agreed to call, and even at that stage, many Russians were looking to him to challenge the very basis of the Communist state, to overthrow the old system and replace it with something new. Tens of thousands were turning out for his election meetings, and I asked him whether he would be able to live up to the people's expectations.

'Some people', he replied with a twinkle in his eye, 'say I am not trying to improve the system, but to abolish it. . . .[pause] . . .I don't go along with that. It is quite another matter, though, that I am in favour of a whole series of things which are – in all senses of the word – revolutionary.' When I asked him whether he wanted to see the one party state replaced by a multi-party democracy, he had another carefully worded answer: 'Multi-party democracy is such a serious thing that we need to hear the views not only of Gorbachov and Yeltsin – that's not important. But if the whole of society wants it, then that is serious. Multi party democracy mustn't be a taboo: the people must be allowed to talk about it, and then in a year or so we draw the necessary conclusions.'

With such ideas, it was certain that Yeltsin would be elected to the new parliament: in the event, he virtually swept the board across the whole of Moscow. In the eyes of the people, Yeltsin was the man who was at last promising to change the old, stagnant political system, while Gorbachov was seen as merely trying to perfect it. The people loved Yeltsin. He was the man who had challenged the Communist juggernaut and had lived to tell the tale, an outsider in a country which loved outsiders. He was 'like them', an ordinary man who drinks, fights and gets angry, but who had the dare-devil courage to take on the system. We once filmed Yeltsin as he was reviewing paratroopers going through their training routine, and after watching a commando leap from a high building into a pool of burning petrol, he made the revealing comment: 'I was just thinking whether I would have jumped into that fire. . . . Well, perhaps not. Although, you know, I'm such a hooligan at heart that maybe I would have jumped after all.' Yeltsin's trump card was always the support he could draw from the streets, from people who also considered themselves 'hooligans at heart'. It was a card he played several times during 1989 and 1990: whenever the party tried to slap him down, he responded by calling thousands of supporters onto the streets. And it was the same card he played with such telling effect on 19 August.

The popular mandate Yeltsin received in the parliamentary elections of 1989 was the turning point, giving him an unassailable moral advantage over Gorbachov, who had never stood for election. At the Party Conference in June 1988, Yeltsin was still pleading with the party for his 'political rehabilitation' after his removal from the Politburo. But by the time of the 28th Party Congress in July 1990, his stock had risen to the point where he could hand in his party card with a public gesture of confidence and disdain. He no longer needed the party, because he had the people instead.

The latter part of 1990, though, was a time of set-backs for Yeltsin. His long-running personal feud with Gorbachov was irritating Western politicians, who felt it was hindering Gorbachov in his efforts at reform and on a visit to Washington Yeltsin was treated with less than due respect by an administration that was remaining stubbornly loyal to Gorbachov. To an outsider, it seemed that the two rival leaders were bent on letting their mutual dislike determine the conduct of their political lives, showing an irresponsible disregard for the fate of the country itself. A temporary truce seemed to have been made at the end of the summer, when they appeared on national television side by side, speaking of their will to cooperate and work together on the economy. The honeymoon was quickly broken, though, when Gorbachov pulled out of his agreement to back the radical Shatalin-Yavlinsky 500 day programme for the transition to a market economy.

The stage was set for an explosive showdown between the two men, and it was eventually sparked by the killings in the Baltics. For many observers, it was Yeltsin's reaction to the January putsch which finally established him as a man of principle and a true defender of reform, freedom and democracy. After years of doubt about his political intent, Yeltsin's undisputed potential had at last found a suitable, honourable cause. Within hours of the sending of troops, he flew to Riga to show his solidarity with the nationalists. He met the Baltic presidents and signed mutual assistance agreements with them. He called on leaders of other republics to form a united front against the Kremlin's threatened use of force.

Yeltsin's alacrity must at the very least have persuaded Gorbachov that military action would provoke an outcry from the republics. And Yeltsin attempted a piece of political theatre that would be re-enacted in his appeal from the top of the tank in August: in a speech that was broadcast throughout the Baltic region, he appealed to Russian troops not to fire on civilians, even if ordered to do so. Those orders, said Yeltsin, were null and void because he had decreed that no Russian troops must ever be deployed in peacetime outside the borders of the Russian Republic. It was a huge bluff, because the troops were in fact commanded by Soviet generals in the Soviet army and were not answerable to him. But his pronouncement made a huge impact in the Baltics and won him wide public support. In Riga, his speech was printed in hundreds of thousands of copies and pasted onto nearly every lamp-post in town: it was in Russian, so the soldiers from Moscow could read it.

As well as his televized demand for Gorbachov's resignation in the wake of the Baltic killings, Yeltsin made a hard-hitting speech to the Russian parliament, calling for a minute's silence for the victims of the troops and demanding that those responsible be brought to justice. To the crowds protesting against the Kremlin's actions, he wrote of the crisis of democracy the President's actions had provoked: 'The goals proclaimed to all the world have been cast aside. Economic reforms are blocked, democracy is betrayed, glasnost is trampled. Lawlessness and dictatorship are being renewed.' He appealed to the people of Russia to join him in the fight to halt the advance of dictatorship: 'We have the strength to stop the forces of reaction. It is within our power to stop the plunge of the Soviet authorities into lawlessness and the use of force. We must show that democracy is irreversible.' It was the beginning of a fight which Yeltsin would see through to its end at the Russian parliament in August.

By the end of January, though, the omens were not propitious. Much of the liberal media which had tried to report the Baltic massacres in an unbiased way had been muzzled or completely silenced. On 1 February Gorbachov's decree allowing military patrols on the streets of Soviet cities came into force; Yeltsin was talking of 'war' against the Soviet leadership; and the country feared that crack-downs like that in the Baltics might be repeated elsewhere. Yeltsin's reaction was ingenious. He knew he had to mount a quick political challenge to Gorbachov before the Soviet President was drawn further into the arms of the hardliners, so he announced that he wanted the creation of a new, executive presidency for Russia which would give the President sweeping powers. The post would be contested in a free, democratic vote of all the people of the Russian republic – and it looked certain to be won by Yeltsin himself.

Gorbachov had a tough decision to make: he could attempt to block the proposal and face the wrath of millions of Russians, or he could acquiesce and see his most dangerous political rival swept to the head of the USSR's largest republic, a position which would inevitably challenge his own authority as President of the Union itself. His inner struggle over the choice was almost fought out on the streets of Moscow. On 28 March Yeltsin had called an extraordinary session of the Russian Congress of People's Deputies to get the new presidency idea on the statute books. He was facing fierce opposition from Communist old believers in the Congress, who were taking every opportunity to blacken his name. But the real challenge was outside the congress hall, where Gorbachov had ordered thousands of police and troops onto the streets to try to prevent a pro-Yeltsin rally planned for that evening.

It looked like the showdown everyone had been expecting and fearing. As the day wore on and the Congress moved slowly towards endorsing Yeltsin's presidency proposals, his supporters began to mass along Gorky Street (since renamed with its old pre-revolutionary, non-Communist title of Tverskaya). Between them and their declared objective of the Kremlin, detachments of riot police moved menacingly into place, blocking their path. As we marched down Gorky Street with Yeltsin's cohorts, bloodshed seemed inevitable. But then, as the first ranks squared up to the line of police and soldiers, the crisis was mysteriously defused. Both sides seem to have received last-minute orders to back off, and while there was some wielding of police batons that night, a stand-off involving more than half a million people was somehow transformed into a major political turning point – the moment when Gorbachov and Yeltsin finally decided to renounce confrontation and work together.

The following day, the Congress resumed but Gorbachov had accepted the new reality and removed his troops from the city centre. Yeltsin made more impassioned speeches inside the hall and suddenly a large group of moderate Communists split away from the party line and came out in his support. Yeltsin's plans for the post of President were adopted without violence and seemingly with the eventual acquiescence of Gorbachov himself.

Compared to the drama of the Congress, the elections, when they took place on 12 June, were an almost low key affair. Yeltsin was faced with three Communist opponents – including the former Prime Minister, Nikolai Ryzhkov – and stood on a platform of radical economic and political reform. While Gorbachov might have been expected to give his backing to one of the Communist candidates, he remained publicly neutral, neither criticizing Yeltsin nor commending him. For his part, Yeltsin stayed uncharacteristically silent about the Soviet President, attacking his old adversary only indirectly as the man who had presided over Russia's descent into penury. In contrast to the misery, the indignity and the despair of life in modern Russia, he – Yeltsin – was offering a chance of change, a chance of social justice, he said, and a chance to return the Russian pride which had been lost under seventy years of Communism. As the votes were counted, it became clear that the Russian people had expressed their overwhelming support for Yeltsin's anti-Communism, and for his devotion to the ideals of democracy, freedom and reform. Yeltsin won by a landslide.

It was a victory which consolidated the liberal forces in Russia and which pulled Gorbachov back from the embrace of the hardliners. Recognizing that Yeltsin now had the democratic backing of the people, Gorbachov had little choice but to seek a formal alliance. Yeltsin had persuaded the Russian parliament to grant him tough new powers, giving him the right to rule by decree; and if it came to a straight choice between obeying Yeltsin's decrees or obeying those of Gorbachov, the elections had shown which way most people would go. The most important expression of the new accord between the two leaders was the agreement over the Union Treaty and Gorbachov's readiness to cede much greater powers to the republics, and it was this swing to the liberals by the President which in the end pushed the plotters into staging the August coup. The victory of Yeltsin at the ballot box had thus contributed to the assault by the hardliners on democracy. But his victory had also given him the mandate, the strength and the courage he needed to resist and ultimately triumph over the gravest challenge to modern Russian democracy.

PART 3

The Denouement

7

Wednesday–Saturday,
21–24 August

The announcement of the deaths of Ilya Krichevsky, Dmitri Komar and Volodya Usov on the public address system of the Russian parliament in the early hours of Wednesday, 21 August marked the height of the coup and the lowest point of liberal morale. The violence and the killings on the barricades were, in retrospect, the turning point which signalled a decisive reversal of fortunes.

The thousands of defenders at the parliament responded to the news by a frantic last-minute effort to complete the makeshift barriers around the building. These had taken on a more solid appearance since the arrival of the tank unit which had abandoned the Yanayev regime and come over to the democrats. Several of the tanks had been incorporated into the barricades, and their gun barrels now protruded from a mass of severed lamp posts, park benches and steel rods. For the *starshii*, the stewards in charge of each sector of the defences, it was a constant struggle to stop over-enthusiastic barricade builders from piling material too tightly around the tanks and thus preventing the guns from manoeuvring.

As soon as the deaths on the streets had been announced, the tank crews had taken their places inside their vehicles and were steadying themselves for battle. For the crowds of civilians, it was a question of final drills and practices, making sure there were no breaks in the human chains encircling the parliament. For the volunteer doctors and nurses in the makeshift field hospitals, it was a time to prepare for the casualties which now looked inevitable.

When the tannoys crackled into life again, everyone expected more news of the Soviet army's advance. But this time the voice that floated through the night was different, more excited, clearly impatient to impart its information: 'Comrades, there is good news. . . .' The crowd of thousands fell completely silent, deeply expectant, straining to catch even the slightest word of encouragement. 'Esteemed defenders, I have to tell you that Pavlov has had a heart attack . . .[a hurried rustling of papers over the tannoy] . . . fellow democrats, I have to tell you he has resigned; but not only that, we believe Yazov is resigning too!

There was just a second of quiet as the news sank in, and then it was uproar, a welling up of sound that took your breath away, as all the emotion which had been repressed behind grim faces and silent lips for so long was unleashed into the depths of the Moscow night. Many of those present did not fully believe the announcement of the resignations (the suggestion that Yazov had gone turned out later to be deliberate disinformation), but all of us wanted to believe it. After two days of unending bad news, it was like water to a man dying of thirst. The celebrations around the camp fires at the front of the parliament were a moment of catharsis. Suddenly, everyone was talking to each other. After hours of reticence and caution, fearing that the man next to you might be a KGB operative or a spy for the plotters working under cover of the night, the constraints seemed to have been lifted. It was all the stewards could do to calm people down and prod them back to their place in the chain. And they were right. For all the chatter and all the speculation about dissension within the ranks of the plotters, there was no proof that they had changed their minds, and no proof that an attack on the parliament was any the less likely.

But by the time dawn broke – the second dawn on the barricades – the belief that an attack would not now happen had taken hold of the crowds. As we ate our breakfasts of bread and sausage, we all felt the worse was over: the coup leaders had ordered the army onto the streets to try to intimidate the democrats, but the lines had held and the defenders of the parliament had not run away. When it came to the moment of decision, the plotters had not had the resolution or the courage to carry through the threats they had made: they had stopped short of an all-out assault on the parliament and Boris Yeltsin was still at large. We all knew we would have to come back again that evening and perhaps in the following days until the coup was finally defeated; but even then we felt that we had all in our small way contributed to the salvation of democracy in Russia.

By mid-morning nothing had been heard from the coup leaders. There were no more news conferences and no official declarations; but neither had there been any confirmation of Pavlov's heart attack, let alone of Yazov's resignation. Most worrying of all, the tanks were still on the streets and the military threat still in place. The city's rumour mill was working overtime, and anxiety was beginning to replace the relief of the early morning.

But at two o'clock in the afternoon, startling reports began to arrive of tank movements on Leningradsky Prospekt (the continuation of Gorky Street where it leaves the Moscow boundary), and this time the tanks were heading not into the city but out of it. Journalists and cameramen sped off in pursuit of the rumour, expecting little more than a wild goose chase. But there on the Leningrad road, exactly as had been reported, were the tanks. They were the same vast columns I had seen drive down Gorky Street and past the Belorussian Station during the previous nights: at that time they had thundered down the hill into town; and I had sat at the wheel of my car in a side street, held back by a militiaman's baton and fearing arrest under the curfew orders. But now it was broad daylight and the armour was churning up the hill, out of Moscow and – we assumed – back to barracks. It was an astounding turnaround.

Tank columns were also reported on the road leading out to Vnukovo, the city's main domestic airport. These sightings were also checked out and found to be correct, but in the centre of town the tanks around the Kremlin were showing no sign of moving. We found out later that they were being left until last for logistical reasons: the withdrawal of the outer regiments was blocking the path of those in the city centre. What we were seeing now were the hundreds of tanks and armoured personnel carriers which had spent the last two days drawn up in fields on the edge of Moscow. We had known the plotters had armour in reserve, but the extent of the forces at their command was frightening even now. The puny number of tanks we had counted on at the Russian parliament bore no comparison.

Moscow Radio now confirmed that a withdrawal had indeed been ordered: the announcement read over the airwaves was signed by Dmitri Yazov, not in his capacity as a member of the plotters' State Emergency Committee, but under his old title of Defence Minister. It was confirmation that the reports of Yazov's resignation by the Russian parliament were indeed premature; but at the same time it was an indication that the Emergency Committee was no longer running the show. Nursultan Nazarbayev, the liberal president of Kazakhstan and an old acquaintance of Yazov, said later that he had repeatedly telephoned the Defence Minister during the coup and had found him worried and uncertain. After the killings on the barricades, Yazov had been hesitating between throwing in the towel and facing criminal prosecution, or gambling on a last desperate attack on the Russian parliament, which would almost certainly bring more casualties without guaranteeing the triumph of the coup leaders. It was the ferocity of the resistance offered by Yeltsin and the democrats which seems to have surprised the plotters and caused them to argue among themselves (although they could hardly have been serious in expecting Yeltsin to cooperate with them, as they had at one point proposed).

Yeltsin himself was still inside the parliament building. He had called an emergency session of all deputies for early Wednesday morning, which had started on time, despite the continued presence of troops on the streets. Many liberal MPs had been in the building for the duration of the siege, and others arrived as the morning wore on. Yeltsin seemed subdued but confident as he addressed the session, making a brief opening statement in which he said he had already received an offer of concessions from the coup leaders. They had accepted his demand for a meeting with Gorbachov to enable him to confirm that the President had not been assassinated, as rumours were now suggesting. He had however refused the plotters' offer to fly him down to the Crimea, where Gorbachov was still under house arrest at his holiday home: the conspirators were proposing that Yeltsin should travel alone, in the company of Anatoly Lukyanov, who was already suspected of being the motivating force behind the coup. This, said Yeltsin, was an unacceptable security risk which left open the possibility of foul play by the State Emergency Committee. Instead, he proposed that the parliament should send a substantial delegation of MPs to the Crimea and that they should report back on their meeting with Gorbachov. This was quickly agreed and the Russian Prime Minister Ivan Silayev was appointed to lead the delegation, which left almost at once for the airport.

Moments later, Yeltsin told the session that he had just been officially informed of the troop withdrawal from the city, an announcement that was met with applause from the hall. But Yeltsin seemed to be waiting for the arrival of further news, and he stepped down from the podium to allow a string of other speakers to take the floor. All those who did so were united in their condemnation of the coup and in calling for the plotters to be arrested and brought to trial. They were, said the deputies, state criminals who should face treason charges and a possible death penalty.

Then Yeltsin interrupted the proceedings with an announcement which caused pandemonium: 'A group of tourists', he said, 'have been spotted on their way to Vnukovo airport.' As he spoke further, it became clear that these 'tourists' were leaving in a great hurry and in the back of large black limousines reserved for the top Kremlin leadership: the plotters were fleeing. Their official motorcade was filmed on the airport road, weaving impatiently through the columns of retreating tanks which they themselves had earlier ordered into action. It was an undignified exit for men who had pretended to supreme power in the Soviet Union, and their dash to escape was uncannily reminiscent of the flight of Nikolai and Elena Ceausescu. Like the Roumanian leaders, the Soviet conspirators were facing retribution from the people they had led to near disaster.

Yeltsin's announcement brought calls from the floor for the coup leaders' capture, to which Yeltsin replied that Russian security police had been despatched in pursuit, but had failed to catch up with the motorcade before it reached the airport. Speculation now began to centre on where the conspirators were heading. Suggestions included central Asia and even Lithuania; the Lithuanians were reported to have said that, if so, they would not be allowed to land. In the end, it transpired that several of the plotters had actually remained in Moscow, and that those who had left were flying down to the Crimea to try to see Mikhail Gorbachov (a move which was later to fuel speculation that the President may himself have taken some role in the coup).

Back in the city, it was mid-afternoon before the tanks around the Kremlin finally began to move out, wheeling through Manezhnaya Square and disappearing down Kalinin Prospekt in clouds of grey smoke. Within minutes of the tanks' departure, the crowds of demonstrators who the previous day had been kept out of the area by the lines of armoured vehicles began to assemble. The people had heard of the plotters' flight; they had seen the tanks leave; and the radio was now announcing that the curfew and the emergency regulations had been lifted. The crowds, though, were still wary: there was little or no chanting, no immediate expression of joy or even of anger against the men who had tried to seize power. For the moment, the people were just happy to be able to walk freely in the shadow of the Kremlin walls without fearing the wrath of the men inside.

The early evening news on Soviet television that Wednesday broadcast the first official confirmation of Mikhail Gorbachov's condition. He was, said the news reader, in good health and had issued a statement confirming his intention to return soon to Moscow. His statement said that he was now in full control of the situation (rather wishful thinking in the circumstances, and a claim that was proved fanciful by subsequent events); he had re-established the telephone communications with Moscow which had been cut off during the coup, and was intending to return to the complete control of his presidential powers in the immediate future. He had, he said, spoken to Yeltsin and other republican leaders, and referred to the coup having been defeated by the 'decisive action of democratic forces in the country' (no mention yet of his debt to Boris Yeltsin). The 'adventurists' behind the putsch would be brought to justice for their actions, and he had taken over full control of the armed forces: henceforth they would obey only the orders of the President (although he still indicated his trust in General Mikhail Moiseyev, the Chief of the Soviet General Staff, who was later removed at Yeltsin's insistence for his involvement in the coup). Gorbachov also said that he had spoken by telephone with George Bush, who had expressed his satisfaction at the ending of the coup, and had told the American President that the 'processes of democratic transformation in the USSR' would be continued. It was the first indication of Gorbachov's mistaken belief that things could carry on as before, in a country where everything was about to change beyond recognition.

The return to something approaching objectivity by the news media removed one of the biggest obstacles that Yeltsin had faced for the past three days. The banning of liberal opinion on television, radio and in the newspapers had left the population virtually uninformed of the reality of the situation in the country. Now the liberals' public voice was returning: on Wednesday night Ivan Laptev, the deputy speaker of the Supreme Soviet, announced on national television that all decrees passed in the brief reign of Gennady Yanayev had been declared invalid and that the leaders of the attempted coup would be sought out and brought to trial.

At the Russian parliament, the defenders had discussed the situation and had concluded that the threat of a hardline backlash still existed. The decision was taken to maintain the vigil for at least one more night, and additional barricades were built on approach roads to the parliament. On the Moskva river alongside the building, barges were towed into place to ward off any possibility of an attack from the water. The mood of the crowds, though, was completely changed from the preceding nights. Now there was singing and dancing around the camp fires in celebration of the victory all believed had been won. When the morning of Thursday came, the crowds had thinned out, but the joy of those who remained was complete: another night had gone by; there had again been no attack on the parliament, and the forces of reaction were in full retreat.

Thursday, 22 August

Mikhail Gorbachov had been scheduled to come back to Moscow from his summer vacation in the Crimea on Monday, 19 August. His return was delayed until the early hours of Thursday, 22 August, just three days late. But he had missed the most important 72 hours in modern Soviet history and it was clear from the moment he stepped off the plane that he was going to find it hard to catch up.

Looking dishevelled and unsteady as he descended the steps of the aeroplane, the President gave the impression of being considerably shaken by his ordeal. He was dressed in an open-necked shirt and a white, unzipped anorak; behind him, blinking in the camera lights as they walked onto the tarmac, were Raisa Gorbachov and their young granddaughter Anastasia who had shared the President's captivity. Gorbachov's first words bore all the hallmarks of a man who was expecting to step back into his old role as leader of the Soviet Union. He immediately tried to claim for himself some of the credit for defeating the coup:

> The main thing is that all we have been doing since 1985 has borne fruit. People and society have changed, and it was this which provided the main obstacle to the adventurists. . . .I congratulate the Soviet people, who have shown responsibility and honour, because they proved the respect they have for those to whom they entrusted power. . . .It is the great victory of perestroika.

While it was true that the long-term factors which prompted people to resist the tanks were indeed the disdain for totalitarianism and the encouragement to independent thought which Gorbachov had initiated, it was only in his later remarks that the President identified the true reason for his salvation from the clutches of the plotters: 'I express my gratitude to the Soviet people; for the principled position adopted by Russia, and to the President of Russia, Boris Nikolaevich Yeltsin.'

Gorbachov, though, was clearly anxious to portray himself in a heroic light, perhaps feeling already that he had been badly upstaged by Yeltsin. He stressed the pressure he had been put under by the conspirators, talking of his isolation from the world, and the blockade from land and sea which had been thrown round his seaside holiday villa. But this was producing little impression compared to the blockade Yeltsin had had to endure. He talked of the coup leaders' attempts to 'break' him and his family, and said he had resisted them at every step. But for Russians, the resistance they identified as defeating the coup was that of Boris Yeltsin.

The putsch, Gorbachov said, must be a lesson to everyone, including the President, politicians and journalists, and he correctly identified the causes of popular unrest which the plotters had tried to play on: 'the problems with food supplies, fuel for the winter, finances, the market situation . . . and the concern over what tomorrow may bring'. But there was a certain complacency in his simply saying that he was 'dealing with these problems'. Even at this early stage it was clear that Gorbachov had not in fact learned the lesson to which he himself had referred.

In his press conference later that day and in a prepared speech on Soviet television, Gorbachov filled in the details of how his arrest had been engineered, and how he had reacted. At the press conference, there was unprecedented applause from the journalists as Gorbachov walked in: he himself was visibly very emotional, halting in his speech and seemingly choking back tears on more than one occasion. He called the coup the greatest test perestroika had had to face in all the years of reform, and he foreshadowed a criticism he would repeatedly have to face in the coming days: 'The organizers of this anti-constitutional coup, those reactionary forces, turned out to be men in the very centre of the leadership, close to the President himself. These were men whom I had personally promoted, believed and trusted.' He seemed genuinely surprised and dismayed that such close colleagues could have led the plot against him: he admitted that he had particularly trusted Yazov and Kryuchkov.

In his account of the drama in the Crimea, Gorbachov described how he had been in his study at his holiday villa on Sunday, 18 August when there was a knock at the door. It was the head of his personal bodyguards, who told him that a delegation had arrived to see him. Gorbachov was suspicious and decided to make inquiries by telephone before receiving the delegation. 'I had a whole series of telephones, a government phone, an ordinary phone, a strategic phone, a satellite phone and so on. I picked up one of them and found it wasn't working. I picked up a second, a third, a fourth, a fifth – they were all the same. Even the internal phone was disconnected. I was isolated.'

Realizing the full seriousness of the situation, Gorbachov called in his wife, daughter and son-in-law. 'I knew there was going to be some sort of attempt at blackmail, or an attempt to arrest me and take me away somewhere. Anything could happen . . . they could have tried all sorts of things, even with my family.' He said his family gave their full backing to his decision not to capitulate to the conspirators.

The delegation turned out to be four envoys sent by Gennady Yanayev's State Emergency Committee with an ultimatum: Gorbachov must either sign a decree introducing a state of emergency in the country, in which case he could stay on as President, but would have to remain in the Crimea; or he must sign over his powers to the Vice President, Gennady Yanayev.

The terms of the ultimatum suggest that the plotters felt they had some grounds for hoping Gorbachov would go along with the state of emergency (in other words, that he would agree to at least a figurehead role in a hardline putsch). Whether he had hinted at this in conversations with them in the past is impossible to tell; but his behaviour over the Baltic crack-down, and his previous cooperation with conservative forces certainly led many to believe that Gorbachov might not be averse to the introduction of tough measures designed to restore discipline, law and order.

We have only Gorbachov's word for how he reacted to the plotters' demands, but the President was absolutely adamant in stressing that he refused point blank to have anything to do with them:

> I told them that they and the men who had sent them were nothing but adventurists. I told them that the course they had decided on would mean their own doom and the doom of our country . . . only someone bent on suicide could propose the introduction of such a totalitarian regime in our country. . . .[I said:] you are trying to play on the problems people are facing today; you are counting on people being tired and being ready to submit to any sort of dictator. . . . But I will only support the politics of agreement, the deepening of reform, and cooperation with the West.

It was a declaration of fundamental importance by Gorbachov: after all the years of his political balancing act, of trying to reconcile hardliners and liberals, he had finally summed up the two sides of the political choice he had long been unwilling to make, and – before the world's press – he had publicly made that choice. Unfortunately for Gorbachov, it had come too late: now it hardly mattered which side he came down on, because power had slipped from him and all the really important decisions would soon be taken by others, chief among them Boris Yeltsin. Gorbachov at this stage was continuing to talk about the need to press ahead with the Union Treaty he had worked out with nine of the republics, not seeming to realize that few of them would now accept any form of subjugation to the centre, even the looser ties the Treaty was proposing. In talking as if the negotiations could simply be picked up from where they were left before the putsch, Gorbachov was again showing that he had not adapted to the new realities of the post coup era.

Having turned down the plotters' demands, Gorbachov seems to have been left in his villa, very much to his own devices. He said his escape routes were blocked by troops and his every move was followed, but there appears to have been little interference in his daily routine and he was allowed to keep his thirty-two bodyguards with him in the house. He was able to listen to the radio, getting news about the situation in the USSR from the Russian Service of the BBC, and he could even watch television (he said he saw the plotters' press conference on the Monday, and joked about Yanayev's nervousness and trembling fingers). They were provided with food, but rejected it in favour of the stocks they already had in the house, in case of an attempt to poison the President.

He had secretly recorded four video messages on the family's home movie camera in the hope of smuggling them out to tell the nation of his plight. In the end, the tapes never left the villa, but we were later shown a copy of them. They begin with Gorbachov's granddaughter Anastasia practising her ballet dancing before the delegation arrived to arrest her grandfather; then they show a haggard-looking Gorbachov speaking straight into the camera and repeating his determination not to collaborate with the coup leaders. Yanayev's claim to have taken power because of the President's ill health was a lie, Gorbachov stated, and consequently all his decrees must be considered null and void.

Eventually, when the coup was on the point of failing, Gorbachov said that a desperate group of plotters turned up on his doorstep (the men who had left in black limousines for Vnukovo airport), but he had refused to speak to them. He did, however, agree to receive Lukyanov, and he initially seems to have had difficulty in believing that his old university friend could have been behind the plot against him. When the Russian parliamentary delegation arrived, Gorbachov said he welcomed them with open arms, expressing his gratitude to them for their conduct during the coup and saying he never again wanted to see a split between himself and the 'other democratic forces'.

But at the same press conference, just a few minutes later, Gorbachov was still defending the Communist party, seemingly unable to accept that it was the party itself which was the coup's organizing force:

> I will do everything possible to drive the reactionary forces out of the party. I believe that on the basis of the party's new programme, it is possible to unite all the progressive and best elements. Therefore, when people speak of the party as a whole being a reactionary force, I cannot agree with that. I know thousands of people in the party's ranks who are true democrats, devoted to perestroika and our struggle. . . . I do not think after all we've been through that we should start organizing witch hunts like they did in the past.

He defended the Central Committee, which later turned out to have sent instructions to party branches in many areas of the country to support the coup; and he defended men like Moscow party boss Yuri Prokofyev who also took an active role in the coup. Even when pressed, the closest Gorbachov came to criticizing the Communist ideal was to say that it had in the past been distorted by Stalinism; and as for his personal position as head of the party, he prevaricated but quoted Lenin and said he would remain firmly devoted to the ideals of socialism. It was hardly a performance which corresponded with the mood of society; and that mood was being seized on and exploited with relish by the country's other leading politician.

In contrast to Gorbachov's low-key return to Moscow, Boris Yeltsin was about to be swept up in a tidal wave of gratitude and adulation. His first public appearance that Thursday morning was to oversee the departure of the tanks which had helped defend him during the siege of the Russian parliament. The troops were sent off with the cheers of the people ringing in their ears, and with their vehicles draped in home-made banners and daubed in slogans by the crowd: one said simply 'Thank you lads', another read 'The pride of Russia'. The celebrations marked the end of the coup, but also the elevation of Yeltsin to a new position of pre-eminence in the Soviet Union. His decisiveness and quick witted determination over the next few days of political manoeuvring were to ensure that Gorbachov would be given little chance to redress the balance.

The Thursday session of the Russian parliament brought further praise and applause for Yeltsin. A standing ovation from the MPs greeted him as soon as he walked onto the stage, and he responded by calling the parliament to its feet to listen with pride to the Russian national anthem. Yeltsin's speech began by celebrating the victory of democracy: he said he had received congratulations from every republic of the Union for the stand Russia had taken, and he himself was unstinting in his praise of those who had defended him and the parliament over the past four days. But he quickly moved on to the theme of retribution for the coup, clearly sensing that decisions taken now would influence the whole balance of political power in the country.

In contrast to Gorbachov's warning against 'witch hunts' in the aftermath of the putsch, Yeltsin seemed ruthless and unmerciful. The plotters themselves had been arrested, he told parliament. Pavlov was indeed in hospital: he had not had a heart attack, but he was suffering from nervous exhaustion. The alcoholic connotations of such a diagnosis raised laughter; but there was no laughter for the next announcement. Another of the conspirators, Interior Minister Boris Pugo, said Yeltsin, had committed suicide when the police arrived to arrest him. In shooting himself, added Yeltsin in a voice bereft of emotion, Pugo had also seriously wounded his wife: 'her present condition is unknown.' Clearly unmoved (Pugo had after all been willing to challenge Boris Yeltsin, so there could be little sympathy for him now), he pressed on: 'All those involved in the coup will be brought to justice and will face the appropriate charges.' He added that there would be no mercy for any official who actively supported the putsch or failed to oppose it.

He ordered the immediate sacking of a long list of local party functionaries, then moved on to the bigger fish. 'I have ordered that Soviet State Television and Radio will be brought under my jurisdiction as President of Russia. I have ordered the sacking of the chairman of State Television, Leonid Kravchenko.' It was Yeltsin's moment of revenge against the hardline Kravchenko, who had enthusiastically broadcast the plotters' propaganda and had kept Yeltsin off the air. *Pravda* and *Sovietskaya Rossiya* were being suspended for the same reasons, said Yeltsin, pending the replacement of their editorial staff. In contrast to Gorbachov's defence of the Communist party's Central Committee, Yeltsin attacked their failure to resist the coup (it was only later discovered that they were its active supporters), and his Prime Minister Ivan Silayev was categorical in his identification of Anatoly Lukyanov as the brains behind the putsch.

Yeltsin was then informed that thousands of well wishers had gathered outside the parliament building, and he announced the suspension of the session, inviting several deputies and aides to come with him to address the crowds. It was the moment of triumph Yeltsin had been seeking: as soon as he appeared on the balcony, the crowd below became a sea of waving hands and tricoloured Russian flags; the roar of cheering could be heard a mile away. Yeltsin was clearly relishing the moment, and he drew wave after wave of applause with a highly charged, emotional speech. The square outside the parliament was being renamed Victory Square, he said, in recognition of the victory that had been won by the people of Russia; 22 August was being declared a national holiday; and, most important of all, Russia's old Soviet flag with its hammer and sickle was being replaced by the pre-Communist tricolour which had become a symbol of freedom.

Again Yeltsin showed his determination to press home his political advantage against Gorbachov and the Communists. It was the party, he said, or at least its Stalinist core, which was to blame for the coup; therefore he had decided to ban all Communist cells in the army and the KGB. He was also determined to win greater freedom from the rule of the central Soviet authorities; he would insist that Gorbachov accept a national government appointed by the republics; and he had ordered the creation of an independent Russian national guard – separate from the Soviet armed forces – to protect Russia against dictatorship. When Yeltsin had suggested a similar move after the Baltic crack down, it had been furiously condemned by Gorbachov and others; but it was now clear to Yeltsin that his status was so high after the putsch that he had virtually a carte blanche to introduce any measures he wished. Gorbachov could no longer stand in his way, and Yeltsin's ruthless streak meant he would exploit his ascendancy to the utmost.

Standing next to Yeltsin on the balcony was General Konstantin Kobets, the Russian Defence Minister who had masterminded resistance operations at the parliament. He praised Yeltsin's courage, saying he had personally asked the Russian President to leave the parliament during the siege and seek refuge in a safer place; but, said Kobets, Yeltsin had replied, 'We will either triumph together, or we will all die together.' Kobets added to the pressure for revenge by saying the plotters should be tried and executed for treason.

Eduard Shevardnadze also addressed the crowd, suggesting that the victims of the tanks should be buried in the Kremlin wall, and recalling his own warning the previous December about the danger of impending dictatorship. 'Don't forget, though, that when I issued my warning, I ended my speech by saying that dictatorship shall not triumph. Today I congratulate you on this great victory. A new democracy has been born: long live democracy!'

When the rally at the Russian parliament ended, the demonstrators flowed down Kalinin Prospekt and into Red Square. The square itself is normally considered hallowed territory and demonstrations had never been allowed to enter it, but on that Thursday afternoon, when nobody was really sure what was and wasn't allowed any more, there was no attempt to stop the people marching past Lenin's mausoleum and demanding the removal of the man who founded the Communist state (a demand which was to grow ever more insistent over the next few weeks). They chanted with gusto, and the name they chanted was not Mikhail Gorbachov, but Boris Yeltsin. If he was listening inside the Kremlin, Gorbachov could have had few illusions about who held the political advantage in the country. The crowd paraded the now ubiquitous Russian flag, once banned by the Communists, and which in only a matter of days would be flying over the Kremlin.

That evening Yeltsin's anti-Communist promptings received their first expression on the streets. Outside the headquarters of the KGB – the infamous Lubyanka – a towering statue of the organization's original founder, Feliks Dzerzhinsky, had struck fear into the hearts of generations of Muscovites. For years, squads of militiamen had patrolled Dzerzhinsky Square to prevent people from even approaching it but now the world had been turned upside down, and when the crowds marched on 'Iron Feliks' no one had the temerity to try to stop them. Over the generations, hatred of the Communists' dreaded security police, whose hand was seen in countless atrocities, had festered in the heart of the nation and tonight the people were determined to take their revenge. The hammers and pick-axes were soon at work; unable to uproot the statue from its base, the bolder members of the crowd clambered onto Dzerzhinsky's shoulders and hung a noose of thick rope around his neck. But despite every effort to topple him, Feliks still stood firm. It was only when Gavriil Popov, the radical mayor of Moscow, despatched a professional wrecking crew with blow torches and circular saws that the effigy finally gave way. In the dark of the night, Dzerzhinsky was driven from the square lying in the back of a lorry with the noose still around his neck, a grotesque echo of the cruel death he had inflicted on so many innocent victims. The marble base of the statue looked certain to end up like the Berlin wall, chipped to pieces by souvenir hunters, but an official from Moscow's Historical Society saved it with a handwritten notice pointing out that the plinth dated from the eighteenth century and should be preserved to support a new statue in the future. The demonstrators showed great restraint in respecting the notice.

The crowds had less respect for the Lubyanka itself, attacking the building, smashing windows and daubing anti-Communist slogans on the walls. Following Yeltsin's lead, the demonstrators shouted their hatred for the KGB, which many now believed had played a central role in the coup. The KGB's chief, the rabid hardliner Vladimir Kryuchkov, was shown on national television that Thursday evening. Sitting in his prison cell awaiting trial for his role in the putsch, he showed little regret: he said that given a second chance, he would do things differently, but the tone of the remark suggested that he meant he would have acted with greater not less ferocity. He expressed the hope that an investigation of the coup might clear his name, but the momentum of anti-Communist hysteria was now reaching the same proportions which had swept away the regimes of eastern Europe, and it was already clear that none of Gorbachov's appeals for restraint were having any effect.

Friday, 23 August

The end of the week brought the political showdown which was to determine the country's future. Gorbachov's efforts to defend the Communist party and the old structure of power had had the predictable effect of hardening the stubborn Yeltsin in his resolve to sweep away the whole edifice. He had invited Gorbachov to appear before the Russian parliament on the Friday afternoon, a meeting which he had clearly planned as a trap for the Soviet President, and which he proceeded to use as a public sanctification of his own ascendancy. The televized confrontation between the two men who held the Soviet Union's future in their hands was to become a moment of the highest political theatre. From being a long-time rival and enemy of Gorbachov, Yeltsin had been turned into the President's saviour; and now his unforgiving character and thirst for self-vindication were to drive him to humiliate the man he had saved from the plotters. Gorbachov appeared remarkably naive and remarkably unprepared for his rival's ferocious assault.

The occasion, though, began encouragingly, with both men talking of the areas of agreement between them. Yeltsin said that at their private meeting that morning, there had been complete accord on matters of personnel and appointments to public positions vacated by sympathizers of the coup, including those in the KGB and the army. (In many cases it later transpired that the 'agreement' was, in fact, the result of Yeltsin imposing his candidate on a reluctant Gorbachov. In the case of the Defence Minister, Gorbachov had initially appointed General Mikhail Moiseyev, only to be told by Yeltsin that Moiseyev had been a collaborator who should be removed. Yeltsin then proceeded to nominate Yevgeny Shaposhnikov, the former air force commander, whose appointment Gorbachov rubber-stamped.)

Gorbachov then took the floor and drew loud applause when he thanked Yeltsin and the Russian deputies for their part in defeating the putsch. But the Soviet President clearly thought he could spend the rest of the meeting recounting his own adventures during the coup in the *Boy's Own* style he had come increasingly to adopt. This drew heckling and jeers from the radical deputies, who wanted to turn the encounter into an occasion to grill Gorbachov and win concessions from him. After repeated booing, Gorbachov turned to the hall and asked: 'What do you want from me? I am telling you what I think; what more do you want?'

The radicals, essentially, wanted blood; and when Gorbachov began to defend some of the ministers whom he had promoted to positions of power before the coup, Yeltsin staged a dramatic piece of theatre. Strolling across the podium, he produced a sheaf of papers and thrust them under Gorbachov's nose, demanding that he read the contents of the documents to the hall. A nonplussed Gorbachov looked at the papers and realized that they were the minutes of a cabinet meeting held on the first day of the coup. They contained incriminating evidence about nearly every member of the government and the way they had welcomed the putsch. All were men Gorbachov had supported, and it was clearly going to be very embarrassing for him to read the minutes out in public. But that is exactly what Yeltsin forced him to do.

The minutes detailed an exchange between the ministers and Anatoly Lukyanov, who had come to quiz them on their loyalty to the putsch leaders. According to the transcript, virtually everyone gave Lukyanov an assurance of their support. Gorbachov found a few ministers who spoke against the coup and tried to defend them: 'Look at this bit,' he pleaded 'Gubenko spoke out against them and resigned in protest. Shcherbakov was critical too . . .' Boos from the floor forced Gorbachov to look up. 'He was critical, wasn't he? . . . Look at this, he did say something against them . . .' But in nearly every case, Gorbachov was forced to accept that the men he had appointed were implicated in the plot.

Some ministers later contested the veracity of the transcript Yeltsin had produced, but whatever the truth, the Russian leader's dramatic ploy had its desired effect and Yeltsin won the first objective he had set himself. Gorbachov's acceptance of defeat was public and it was humiliating: 'As a result of this, I have decided that the whole government must resign . . . we must choose a new one, checking all the candidates' loyalty to democratic principles . . . and with the republics' participation in selecting the ministers. . . .

Having forced Gorbachov into acknowledging that his own ministers were implicated in the coup, some deputies went on to accuse the Soviet President himself of being involved, quoting remarks to that effect reportedly made by Anatoly Lukyanov. 'That is nonsense,' stormed Gorbachov. 'Some plotters will try to think up any old rubbish to get themselves off the hook. But I gave them nothing; I agreed to nothing at all! If Lukyanov says this, then he is a criminal. . . . I never conferred with Lukyanov at any stage!'

Throughout the extraordinary spectacle which unfolded on the platform, Gorbachov showed himself to be increasingly out of touch with the radical mood of the parliament, and of the Russian people. He began by defending the Supreme Soviet (the Presidium of which, under the leadership of Lukyanov, was later shown to be deeply implicated in the coup). He then tried to argue for Lukyanov to be given a chance to defend himself; and he told the booing deputies that the aftermath of the putsch must not be turned into a campaign against the Communists. 'I cannot agree that the CPSU is a criminal party. It has reactionaries in it . . . and they must be dealt with. But I will never agree that we should throw out genuine, good Communists. Some Communists fought to rescue me in these days, while others must answer for their actions. But I won't label millions of workers as criminals . . . I won't!'

Sensing the mood of the chamber, Yeltsin's hawk-like instincts told him it was time to move in for the kill. In a second piece of theatre, he fixed Gorbachov in his sights and asked him to confirm publicly that he had agreed to endorse retroactively all decrees issued by Yeltsin during the coup. Gorbachov mumbled something about an understanding they had reached 'not to give away all our secrets'. But Yeltsin was already one step ahead, demanding to know if the agreement included the transfer of all property rights and resources previously controlled by the Kremlin to the jurisdiction of Russia. 'You won't catch me in that trap,' responded Gorbachov, 'there will have to be a decision after the Union Treaty is signed.'

And then Yeltsin made the gesture which may well have sealed the fate of Communism. 'On a lighter note,' he said quietly, looking down at a piece of paper lying on the table in front of him, 'I will now sign a decree banning the functioning of the Communist party of the Russian Republic.' There was immediate and prolonged applause. Yeltsin held aloft the decree, showing his signature on it; while Gorbachov struggled to make himself heard. When he did so, it was a bumbling answer, reflecting how taken aback he had been by Yeltsin's thunderbolt: 'I am sure the Supreme Soviet will not agree to that,' he stammered 'If the Russian Communist party backed the plotters, I would agree with your decree . . . but to ban the RCP would be a major mistake.'

By now, though, it was too late. The idea of banning the Communist party (albeit just the Russian branch of it, not the CPSU) had been uttered in public. What is more, it had received a tumultuous welcome from the Russian deputies; and, most important of all, it had been heard on television by millions of ordinary people, most of whom welcomed the proposal with joy.

The spectacle at the Russian parliament ended with Yeltsin and Gorbachov standing shoulder to shoulder on the podium and talking of how much they needed to work together as defenders of democracy. But the show of unity seemed hollow. How could Yeltsin, who was pressing for the banning of the Communist party, work with Gorbachov who was defending it? One of them would have to back down, and it seemed clear even on the Friday evening that it would not be Yeltsin.

Within hours of the drama at the Russian parliament session, Yeltsin's allies were moving to make his decree a reality. Gavriil Popov ordered militia units to visit Communist party branches throughout the city and evict the occupants. When the police arrived, the reaction from the *apparatchiks* was incredulous. These were men whose right to rule had been enshrined in the Soviet constitution as recently as six months ago; they had expected to stay in power forever; they thought they had jobs for life. At several party branches there were sharp arguments with the militia, but in the end the Communists obediently packed up their briefcases, closed the office door and left. Once the bureaucrats had been removed, the police were under orders to seal all their premises. Yeltsin was eager to secure for himself any evidence which might incriminate the party as an organization in the planning of the coup and he did not want to allow time for documents to be removed or destroyed. At the local party organizations, doors were padlocked and covered with the official seals of the Russian Federation. But at the Central Committee building, where the Moscow party had its headquarters, there were further humiliations for the Communists. As they were driven out of the their offices, the functionaries were forced to run the gauntlet of envoys from the Russian parliament and their enthusiastic helpers from the general public. Before being allowed to walk out of their own front door, the *apparatchiks* were made to open their briefcases and empty their pockets to prove they were not removing any possible evidence. Once the offices inside had been vacated, Boris Yeltsin's emissaries moved in to start searching their desks.

Late on the Friday evening, there was another blow for the already tottering CPSU. In a written statement, the liberal president of Kazakhstan, Nursultan Nazarbayev, announced that he had found evidence of a draft resolution by the Soviet Central Committee, expressing the party's official support for the coup. Nazarbayev said he was quitting the party and he urged all democrats to do the same.

Saturday, 24 August

Saturday is the day on which the Russian Orthodox Church buries its dead, and the 24th was when the funeral in public honour of the three young men killed on the barricades was to take place. The funerals of two of the victims, Dmitri Komar and Volodya Usov would anyway have taken place that day, but the third victim, Ilya Krichevsky, was Jewish, and it took much persuasion from the Russian authorities and Ilya's friends to convince his parents that they should accept the break with Jewish tradition and allow their son to be buried on a Saturday, at the same time as his fellow victims. Ilya's mother, clearly distraught, said her son had been at home on the Tuesday evening listening to news of events in the city on Boris Yeltsin's short wave radio station. He was a studious boy who had never been involved in politics, but on hearing Yeltsin's appeal for volunteers to help defend the Russian parliament, he had simply put on his jacket and run out into the night. His mother wept as she recalled the moment: hardest of all to bear was that her son had never said goodbye. She felt she could only be reconciled to his death by a personal message from Boris Yeltsin, a message that seems to have been forthcoming, and in the end she agreed to Ilya being buried on the Saturday.

The collective funeral of the three young men moved the whole nation. From early morning, crowds gathered in Manezhnaya Square outside the Kremlin, where the funeral procession was due to begin. The coffins were displayed on a common bier and a seemingly endless line of people filed past to pay their last respects. By the appointed time, tens of thousands had packed into the square. They were the same people who in the past had come here to protest against the Communist authorities and to demand greater freedom and democracy. Now they had come to mourn those who had died in winning their common victory over the forces of reaction. Grieving relatives of the dead carried their portraits and Russian tricolours draped with black silk. Afghan veterans turned out to honour Volodya Usov who had fought with them in the forgotten war; and President Gorbachov, his voice choked with emotion, thanked the men whose sacrifice had contributed to his salvation. Gorbachov's tears were certainly genuine as he told the crowds that the three had 'given everything' in the cause of democracy, but he must also have realized that their devotion – and that of the thousands now packed into Manezhnaya Square – was not to him, but to Boris Yeltsin. It may well have been at that moment that he steeled himself for the epoch-making decision he was to announce later that day.

While the Soviet President left to ponder his political future, the crowds moved off in a vast funeral procession along Kalinin Prospekt, the route already lined with rows of sympathizers seven and eight deep. It was an outpouring of public grief unseen in Moscow since the funeral of Andrei Sakharov, and it confirmed that – like Sakharov – the three victims of the tanks would enjoy the status of martyrs and heroes. When the head of the march reached the intersection with the Garden Ring where the men died, it paused in respectful silence. The place of the tragedy on the barricades had already been turned into a shrine to their memory, with flowers piled high and new ones brought daily.

At the Russian parliament, the mourners gathered to hear a speech by Boris Yeltsin, the man for whom they all had been ready to die just a few days earlier. Yeltsin respected the solemnity of the occasion: there was no rabble-rousing and no political campaigning. The emotional high-point of his speech was his address to the parents of the dead: 'I appeal to you, parents of Volodya, of Dmitri and Ilya, to forgive me. Forgive me, your President, that I was unable to save and protect your sons.' There was no objective reason for Yeltsin to ask forgiveness, but asking forgiveness of each other is what Russians do before taking Communion, and Yeltsin was appealing to the deep religious and emotional ties which bind the Russian nation. Many present and watching on television felt it was a moment of spiritual rebirth for their country: a man who had nothing to answer for was accepting the burden of responsibility in contrast to the decades of Communist misrule where few could be found to take responsibility for the darkest of crimes.

As Ilya Krichevsky was laid to rest to the sound of a Jewish lament; and Dmitri Komar and Volodya Usov were accompanied to the grave by the Patriarch of the Russian Orthodox Church, political processes were maturing whose outcome was soon to echo around the world. The first indications of the momentous events that were about to happen came in the early evening, when the independent Interfax News Agency announced that it had been told Gorbachov was rethinking his position on the future of the Communist party and was considering stepping down as General Secretary. Interfax is not an official Kremlin mouthpiece but it has good contacts in the party hierarchy.

A phone call to Gorbachov's spokesman Vitaly Ignatenko quickly confirmed that something was afoot: 'I can neither confirm nor deny suggestions that Gorbachov is going to announce a ban on the Communist party: you must listen to his announcement on television tonight.' It was one of those phrases which officially give away nothing, but which in fact tell the whole story. Ignatenko later reported that he had spent much of the day with Gorbachov as the President struggled with his conscience, bringing himself slowly and painfully to the conclusion that the party which had made him, and which he had served for decades, had so discredited itself in the eyes of the people that it no longer deserved to exist. 'The time had come,' said Ignatenko, looking back on the events of Saturday, 'when the facts about the secret rebellion [of the party against Gorbachov] became more and more widely known . . . Gorbachov was moving all the time towards the conclusion that the party leadership could no longer be part of the system of perestroika. In fact, it had betrayed him.' Gorbachov, he said, had come back from the Crimea having resolved to abandon his party post and put an end to the existence of the Communist party Central Committee.'

With the advantage of hindsight, Ignatenko was doing his best to put Gorbachov's actions in the best light. The President clearly had not decided to abandon the party when he came back from the Crimea. He had spent all day Thursday and Friday trying to defend it, and it was only after much prompting from Yeltsin and the Russian people that he finally took his decision. What had happened that Saturday morning, though, was that files and records from the sealed Central Committee building had been brought to Gorbachov, revealing the true extent of the party's support for the coup. Telegrams and circulars containing instructions on how best to help the plotters' cause had been sent to party branches around the Soviet Union, and these had not been destroyed by the functionaries before they were driven out of the building. The evidence of their treachery was now in the hands of the President. There had been a personal blow, too, with the confirmation that Anatoly Lukyanov had taken an active role in leading the coup, and had been suspended from his post as speaker of the Supreme Soviet. More than anyone, Lukyanov had long been close to Gorbachov, and forty years of political comradeship had made the President trust his old university friend both as a person and as a Communist. With Lukyanov too turning out to be a traitor, Gorbachov must have felt that the whole party had been rotten to the core.

During the course of Saturday afternoon, Gorbachov had received the new American ambassador, Robert Strauss, and had presumably told him in advance of the decision he was about to announce. Then he went to his office in the Kremlin and recorded his television speech. The President's address was short and it confirmed what we had learned during the evening: in light of the events of the past week, Gorbachov felt he could no longer remain as General Secretary of the party; and, what is more, he was recommending that the CPSU Central Committee should dissolve itself. He added wistfully that he still hoped the 'healthy elements' of the party, its democrats and its reformers, could band together to form a new movement dedicated to perestroika. But for Soviet Communism, seventy-four years of political domination had come to an end in six days of whirlwind drama.

PART 4

The Consequences

8

Why Did the Coup Fail?

Attempts to seize power in the Soviet Union are not new. The August coup differs simply in that it did not succeed. Stalin came to power despite Lenin's dying wish to the contrary because he managed to dominate the party bureaucracy and win control of the formal levers of power. Whoever controlled the top Communist bodies also controlled by definition the vast administrative structure which filtered down into all levels of society and gave the men at the top the assurance they needed that their commands would be carried out to the letter. Control of the highest party organs also brought the obedience of the army, militia and state security forces, which could be relied upon to impose the will of the Kremlin if its writ were ever challenged. It was a web of party domination radiating out from the Kremlin and giving the centre an iron grip on the country.

In 1964 the overthrow of Nikita Khrushchev demonstrated the same principle at work. The plans for his removal were hatched among the Communist hierarchy, who secretly sought and won the backing of the party's ruling bodies. Once they had been won over, the actual transfer of power became a formality. In an archetypal palace coup led by Mikhail Suslov, the party's Ideology Secretary, and by Leonid Brezhnev, Khrushchev was called before the Central Committee Presidium, made to listen to a long list of complaints about his conduct and forced into signing his resignation. The Central Committee as a whole, whose backing Suslov had already ensured, endorsed the decision the following day. The end of Khrushchev's decade of sporadic reform had thus been brought about by a few men in a smoke-filled room in the Kremlin.

The 1991 plotters were clearly following the same route and there are illuminating parallels between their actions and those of the

Suslov-Brezhnev clique. In 1964 the conspirators had become increasingly infuriated by Khrushchev's unpredictable swings between
reform and reaction, and by his constant changes which undermined
the privileges and well-being of the party bureaucrats. As in 1991, it
was this last consideration which united the powerful *apparat* against
their leader. Suslov and Brezhnev prepared their coup by securing
the support of the top party leadership, including the Defence and
Interior ministers, and were thus certain that the armed forces and
the state security organs were with them. As in 1991, they chose
the moment when the General Secretary was out of Moscow on
vacation at the Black Sea, summoning him back to face the Central
Committee and to sign his own resignation. In 1991 the plotters
actually took their demands to the General Secretary's holiday home,
but the pretext they used to remove him was the same: 'resignation
for reasons of health'. Khrushchev put up something of a fight, but
agreed in the end to step down. Gorbachov refused, but according
to the 1964 scenario that should have been no great obstacle to the
conspirators: in their reasoning, it needed only the agreement of the
party leadership and bureaucracy to effect a coup, because that is
where ultimate power lay. Khrushchev understood that when he
agreed to go quietly; but Gorbachov realized that some important
changes had taken place since 1964, and that is why he decided to
hold out.

The Yanayev clique had made crucial miscalculations. The first
was their failure to secure the backing of the entire party. Unlike
Suslov and Brezhnev, the 1991 plotters had not made sure in advance
that they could get the endorsement of the whole Central Committee
if it came to a vote. The 'healthy elements' Gorbachov was fond of
referring to did apparently exist, and Lukyanov and the others were
forced to postpone the calling of a plenum (the gathering of all the
Central Committee members, which was theoretically necessary to
remove the General Secretary).

The Supreme Soviet was another wild card for the Yanayev clique.
In 1964 it had been a rubber-stamp body which was certain to endorse
whatever the party decided, but in 1991 it had opinions of its own.
An early session would have allowed embarrassing radical deputies
to speak publicly in condemnation of the coup, and Lukyanov used
every excuse possible to put off its convocation. In theory, the
agreement of the Congress of People's Deputies was also necessary
to endorse the change of State President (it was the only body with
the authority to appoint or remove a president: when he created the

post, Gorbachov had clearly had this in mind as a means of making his removal from power more difficult).

The changes in the top bodies of party and state which made it harder for the plotters to suborn them were all the result of Gorbachov's own reforms. It was he who had introduced the democratic elements which had the potential to resist the conspirators, and he who had broken the old certainty that whoever controls the centre controls the country. But if other things had been equal, all the changes in the formal organs of power would have made little difference. For the plotters were able to win enough backing in the Central Committee to send instructions in its name to party branches, and to formulate the draft resolution of support for the coup, discovered later by Nursultan Nazarbayev.

There was, however, one change between 1964 and 1991 which Yanayev and the others seem to have ignored completely, but which Gorbachov was prepared to gamble on. It was the factor which marked the essential difference between the removal of Nikita Khrushchev and the attempted removal of Mikhail Gorbachov; and it was first pointed out to me several months before the coup by Khrushchev's own son, Sergei Khruschchev, who is now a political writer and analyst. In April 1991 we had met at his father's graveside to discuss the possibility of a hardline attempt to remove Gorbachov from power. When I asked him whether the present Soviet leader could be ousted in the same way as his father, he replied that it was certainly possible but that he did not think it would happen. 'My father's reforms were carried out within the rules of the Communist system and he could therefore be removed by that system. . . . Gorbachov's reforms have changed the system.' The crucial difference, he said, was that Gorbachov had changed the structure of the state to involve the people in the political process, and that anyone who wanted to seize power in 1991 would have to reckon with them as an important element in the political equation. It was no longer enough to change the hand on the levers of power and assume that control of the country had been passed to new owners: any pretender to the leadership of the USSR would have to change not only the party organs in the Kremlin, they would have to change the people as well.

Unfortunately for the plotters, they went ahead with their coup as if it were still 1964, when the people were expected simply to accept the changes in the Kremlin and get on with their lives under new management. In planning the coup, the plotters seemed to have looked no further ahead than their first steps, which they believed would be decisive. Under the logic of the old Soviet Union, organizing the physical removal of the General Secretary from the political stage should have been enough to ensure the triumph of the new regime, and the public (in the form of well-organized party branches, public organizations and factory collectives) should have showered them with telegrams of congratulations.

After they had secured Khrushchev's resignation, the Suslov-Brezhnev clique had sent tanks into Moscow, but the aim was not the seizure of power – power had already been seized when the General Secretary stepped down – but a threatening presence to ensure law and order on the streets. Yanayev and the others seem to have reasoned in the same way when they sent their troops out, never expecting to have to use them to crush any concerted rebellion (this was an important factor in their attitude when the final choice had to be made over an assault on the Russian parliament). So convinced were the plotters that they had done enough to assume real power that on the Monday of the coup they suggested to Boris Yeltsin that he sign a cooperation accord and collaborate with them. They presumably believed that Yeltsin had been convinced, like them, that the State Emergency Committee now enjoyed absolute power and that they had taken charge of the country, when in fact all they controlled was the brittle skeleton of a power structure.

Even so, if it had not been for the show of defiance at the Russian parliament, it seems likely that Yanayev would have consolidated his hold on power and led the country back into the dark ages of Communist orthodoxy. It was the resistance of the people which ensured the defeat of the coup, although in the final analysis, it was not the Russian people as a whole who resisted the putsch. The fifty thousand or so who turned out at the Russian parliament were only a tiny percentage of the Moscow population, and it was always within the military means of the plotters to storm the parliament, arrest Yeltsin and declare victory. That is what the defenders of the parliament expected them to do, and the conspirators' failure to act has raised many questions.

The men behind the coup had not been averse to spilling blood in the past, as the January experience in the Baltics testified. But now they not only left their number one opponent at large, they also left him with telephone lines, electricity and satellite communications to contact world leaders like George Bush and John Major. Instead of securing practical control of the country and then declaring themselves the new leaders of the state, the conspirators did it the other way round. When they did try to impose emergency measures, it was done in a haphazard way which left the potential opposition considerable room for manoeuvre. They introduced an ,information black-out, but allowed Yeltsin's short wave broadcasts to continue; and they failed to jam foreign radio stations like the BBC Russian Service or the Voice of America, which continued to undermine their own propaganda. They made no moves to sack ministers or other officials and replace them with their own people. They posted military patrols at key installations, but they did not enforce the curfew with any ruthlessness.

By failing to keep people off the streets, they thus allowed resistance to grow; by failing adequately to terrorize the population, they encouraged waverers to join in demonstrations; by allowing their own orders to be flouted, they undermined any authority they might have had. Why did men like Yazov and Kryuchkov, who had organized coups in Afghanistan, Africa and elsewhere, suddenly lack the knowledge or the will to act effectively when it most mattered? Kryuchkov had taken part in the imposition of martial law in Poland in December 1981, so why did he not repeat the exercise in 1991 with the same efficiency he had shown ten years earlier?

Leaving aside the conspiracy theory of history, which holds that the coup was a piece of theatre staged with the knowledge of and for the benefit of Gorbachov and/or Yeltsin, there are several possibilities. The plotters may simply have been the 'no hopers' Gorbachov described them as, unable to stage an efficient coup and unable to organize the military action it demanded. When Aleksandr Yakolev was asked later why he thought the State Emergency Committee had been so ineffective, he just laughed and said 'Fools. . . .fools'. This explanation goes together with the stories of heavy drinking among the conspirators and the reports that Yanayev was in an alcoholic stupor when the police arrived to arrest him. But it does not account for Anatoly Lukyanov, who kept his head throughout the coup and was clearly capable of organizing whatever measures needed to be taken. Nor did anybody cast any doubt on the determination and military sang-froid of Dmitri Yazov.

There is also the suggestion of a split in the army which prevented a concerted assault, and indeed some troops did defect to the democrats. These, though, were such a minute proportion of the forces available to Yazov that in purely military terms they would have made little or no difference, except for increasing the potential for casualties in a battle for the Russian parliament. (A few tanks and part of a parachute regiment would not have lasted long against the massed ranks of armour we saw on the day the Soviet army withdrew from town.)

What might have played a bigger role in the plotters' mind was the potential for conflict within the army once the parliament had been seized and the initial campaign was over. If the storming of the parliament brought heavy loss of life, it would be certain to spark further pockets of resistance throughout the country: radical centres like Leningrad would be most unlikely to surrender quietly, and the Baltics too would rise in arms. If so, the Soviet army would have to fight an internal campaign on many fronts. Soldiers would have to be ordered to open fire on their compatriots and the threat of civil war would loom. Under such circumstances, troops who might have followed instructions to storm the Russian parliament without too many qualms would be put under much greater pressure, and the cohesion of the army would be unlikely to last. A widespread campaign fought in numerous locations would mean middle-ranking officers, many of them younger and more radical than the old, hardline generals, would have to be called on to take the strategic military decisions. Control of the war would pass out of the hands of 'reliable' commanders at the top of the military structure and into those of others who would be more likely to break ranks.

All these factors must have been in Dmitri Yazov's thoughts when he talked by telephone to Nursultan Nazarbayev during the coup and debated whether or not to attack the Russian parliament. There can have been little doubt in Yazov's mind that he would have won the initial battle; he may, though, have balked at being drawn into a continuing war which he would have been more than likely to lose. This explanation – that the plotters had not bargained for an extended campaign, and realized that they would lose it if they embarked upon it – is given added credibility by Yanayev's reported reaction to the news of the three deaths on the barricades. He is said to have exclaimed, 'Oh, no. We didn't expect this', a reaction which supports the suggestion that the plotters had hoped to take over power in the Suslov–Brezhnev manner: they had banked everything on a palace coup which would transfer power to them without having to fight for it on the streets. When it transpired that they would have to battle for power over an extended period, and when they saw how public opinion was turned against them, they drew the correct conclusion that this was a long-term battle they could not win.

There was also the issue of international opinion. Yanayev would have assumed rightly that a speedy assumption of power by the new regime would have to be accepted by the rest of the world as a *fait accompli*. He may have allowed for initial outrage and possibly the withdrawal of short-term economic aid; but he would also have known that Western politics operates on the basis of self-interest, and that Washington or London would be unlikely in the long term to jeopardize the gains of continued dialogue with Moscow for the sake of a little moral outrage over the way power was transferred within the Kremlin. On the first day of the coup, George Bush was already offering encouraging signs by saying that his 'gut instinct' was that acting president Yanayev 'has a certain commitment to reform'. They were the words of a leader who was calculating that he might have to work with the man in the future, and not wanting to offend him by too much criticism.

But Yanayev would also have known that the credit he might enjoy in the eyes of the world was only good as long as his accession to power was speedy and relatively bloodless. Any protracted power struggle would allow the West to pick its candidate among the men battling for supremacy, and if it came to a choice between him and Mikhail Gorbachov, or him and Boris Yeltsin, the West would not be picking Gennady Yanayev. Yanayev knew he would have to remove the old leadership in a way which could be made to look acceptable to the West (hence all the references in his initial announcement to the articles of the Soviet constitution under which Gorbachov was being replaced), and then intimidate the population into accepting this without actually resorting to bloodshed.

In 1964 it might well have worked, but under the new conditions of Soviet society it was far from certain, and the three deaths on the Tuesday evening virtually ended Yanayev's hopes. The killings had taken place outside the US embassy; and the longer the resistance to the troops continued, the more world opinion was likely to turn against the conspirators. With Yeltsin playing the role of democracy's last defender and talking to Bush and Major from the besieged parliament, Yanayev must have realized that his chances were fading. For all his bluster about Moscow being able to dispense with foreign economic assistance, he knew full well that a loss of Western goodwill would spell economic disaster for his regime. Unlike Chile, the USSR did not enjoy the economic independence and well-being which would allow a dictator to abuse human rights without having to worry about the threat of Western sanctions. He could not afford to massacre civilians at the Russian parliament, within earshot of the American embassy, while still begging Washington for grain and trade credits.

In sum, the most likely explanation for the plotters' indecision and seeming lack of nerve is that they were never prepared for anything other than a palace coup, which would all be over in a matter of hours. They expected a repeat of 1964, and when that failed to materialize they were lost. They had failed to allow for the public resistance which interrupted their plans, and when the stand-off continued, they found that the odds were ever more stacked against them. In the end, the one positive item on their moral balance sheet is that they accepted they were beaten and threw in the towel before further bloodshed occurred: more ruthless conspirators might have reckoned that they were doomed anyway, and decided to take as many of their opponents with them as possible.

The failure of the August coup was the catalyst for potentially the most far-reaching changes in the Russian empire since the 1917 revolution. Yet the putsch initially seemed destined to return the country to the well-worn rut of Russian history. Periodic attempts at reform in Russia and the Soviet Union in the past had, without exception, provoked a conservative reaction which brought them to a premature end. Khrushchev's overthrow was just a more recent example of the process which had terminated the innovations of the New Economic Policy in the 1920s, the reforms of Prime Minister Pyotr Stolypin before the First World War, and even the attempts at change by the reformist tsars.

The consistent failure of democratic reforms to take root in Russia had promoted a fatalism about the way the country was run. The belief that Russia, and later the Soviet Union, was so unruly, divided and unmanageable that it needed the iron grip of a dictator was widely accepted as an immutable law. Indeed, whenever attempts were made to introduce Western-style democracy, or even to relax slightly the power of the centre, the country's inherent centrifugal forces (nationalism, revolt, hatred of an oppressive system, and the economic egotism of richer regions) would begin to tear it apart. Such centrifugal tendencies had surfaced violently as soon as Gorbachov began to relax the iron grip of the old Communist system, and it was argued that parliamentary democracy could never succeed in a country where rival parties would be created on strongly regional lines: their only policies would be to demand independence for their own territories and they would have a strong aversion to participating in any form of central parliament. Modern Russia, ran the theory, was an artificial empire created by the use of force against different nationalities, held together by force, and doomed to explode as soon as that force was removed.

The classical pattern was that attempts at reform were crushed by the powers of reaction, so when the tanks appeared on 19 August, it seemed as if the pattern was about to repeat itself. But Vladimir Lenin had a view of history which goes some way towards explaining why the reactionary forces failed in 1991 where they had triumphed in the past. Lenin's theory was that historical processes – in particular, the path towards revolution – often progress on a 'two steps forward, one step back' basis. Thus, although it might seem that a period of change has been totally negated by its ultimate reversal, in reality society never regresses quite to the point it was at before the reforms were attempted. The Polish Solidarity activist, Adam Michnik, was fond of applying Lenin's theory to his own country's progress away from Communism: the periodic Polish revolts, in 1956, 1970, 1980–1, all seemed to end in failure, but, said Michnik, each one had left its imprint on society, so that the next time the nation made a bid for liberation, its starting point would be one step further down the road to its historical goal. Finally, in 1988–9, Poland along with the rest of eastern Europe made the vital step which took it 'over the edge'; but that final step would never have been possible without the attempts at progress and reform in previous years, which had blazed the trail.

In August 1991 Russia too 'stepped over the edge'. Attempted reforms in earlier years had been crushed by the forces of conservatism; progress even in the Gorbachov era had been marked by swings between reform and reaction; but each seeming reverse had left society more demanding and more aware. By the time August came, the nation had already stepped beyond the point of no return and all the plotters' efforts could not force it to take the 'one step back' which had accompanied the end of reformist experiments in the past. In fact, the failure of the coup had precisely the opposite effect: instead of ensuring the reversal of the liberal reforms which the plotters opposed, it gave the push that was needed to ensure their ultimate and dramatic triumph. The failed putsch was the immediate catalyst for the defeat of Soviet Communism and the dissolution of the Russian empire.

9

Was Gorbachov Behind the Coup?

The public leaders of the August coup were quickly rounded up and put behind bars. Others who worked behind the scenes to help the plotters were also tracked down and arrested. Politicians and officials who did not actively oppose the putsch were sacked from their jobs. But, as with all political crimes committed in the public arena, there was much speculation in the days after the coup that other, as yet unpunished participants existed within the highest echelons of the leadership. According to the Soviet rumour mill, the men who pulled the trigger had been caught, but the man who gave the orders had not.

The public finger of suspicion was pointed relentlessly at Gorbachov. When the President appeared before the Russian parliament on the Friday after the coup, the allegations that were on so many lips were put to him openly, in front of a television audience of millions. Not surprisingly, Gorbachov responded to the deputies' suggestions with an angry, contemptuous denial. In all his published accounts of the drama in the Crimea, the first point he always made – and then insisted on repeating – was that he did not collaborate with the plotters and steadfastly resisted all their attempts to make him do so. For the President to allow even a shadow of a suggestion that he was implicated in the coup would have been tantamount to political death, and could have led to him joining his former colleagues in the Soviet leadership in their prison cells.

The Soviet public received Gorbachov's denials with a certain scepticism. The most convinced exponents of the Gorbachov conspiracy theory insisted that the circumstantial evidence and the presence of a compelling motive were proof enough of his guilt. While the case may not ultimately be as watertight as they suggest, there are unexplained factors in the behaviour of both the plotters and the President which demand investigation.

The circumstantial evidence centres largely on the inefficiency of the conspirators and the apparent inability of men who had directed coups and uprisings abroad to repeat the exercise in their own country. For the conspiracy theorists, this was an indication not of stupidity, but of duplicity.

The plotters' lack of success in isolating Boris Yeltsin and his colleagues, in cutting off phone lines, suppressing public dissent and controlling the flow of information was detailed in the previous chapter. Yeltsin himself had been allowed to fly into Moscow early on the Monday morning of the coup: no attempt had been made to arrest him on arrival, and he was allowed to travel first to his dacha, meet the Russian Republic leadership and then drive on to the Russian parliament. He was not picked up by the troops, and neither was Anatoly Sobchak, the radical anti-coup mayor of Leningrad, who was allowed to fly home unmolested from Moscow.

Muscovites were aware of the State Emergency Committee's failings, because they could hear foreign radio stations and even watch the uncensored broadcasts of CNN beaming pictures of the events on the streets of their city back into the Soviet Union. The Emergency Committee had taken control of the Soviet TV tower early on the Monday morning, and could easily have 'pulled the plug' on CNN's transmissions, just as it could have done with all foreign broadcasters. The more suspicious members of the population began to ask themselves why the Committee was being so lackadaisical; and many thought they had found the answer in Yanayev's press conference. When asked about Gorbachov's position, he said he hoped that 'when the President had recovered his health, he might return to his duties'.

The hint of complicity was increased when Gorbachov himself revealed the conditions he was held in during his detention in the Crimea, including the fact that he was allowed to keep his thirty-two bodyguards with him. Gorbachov insisted he had been isolated and cut off from the world, and yet virtually in the same breath admitted that he had been able to listen to the BBC and to watch Yanayev's press conference on television. He said his phones were all cut off, but later talked of speaking to Boris Yeltsin on the Wednesday afternoon. And when the coup was in tatters and the plotters took off from Moscow airport, they did not fly off to safety in somewhere like Iraq (which had publicly welcomed Yanayev's seizure of power), but flew instead to the Crimea, to try to rejoin Mikhail Gorbachov. Their motives were never clearly elucidated, and public suspicions about Gorbachov's role were redoubled. Even if Lukyanov and the others had run to the Crimea merely to try to strike a deal with the man they had supposedly deposed, their behaviour suggests they considered Gorbachov sympathetic enough to their cause to consider a pardon. But subsequent developments raised the possibility of even closer complicity.

Lukyanov himself, in the days between the end of the coup and his eventual arrest on charges of masterminding the putsch, made repeated appearances in the lobby of the Supreme Soviet, where he told his version of events to journalists and anyone else willing to listen. When pressed about Gorbachov's role, Lukyanov replied, 'Mikhail Sergeevich knew about everything. He was kept informed.' (These were the remarks which the deputies in the Russian parliament were later to use to challenge Gorbachov to his face.)

The logic behind this version, according to popular belief, was that Gorbachov had planned the coup together with the plotters. The reasoning was simple: having committed himself to the new Union Treaty, he had realized that he was consigning the Union to the scrap heap and, more importantly, reducing his own powers as Union President to the figurehead role of a constitutional monarch. He had therefore come to the conclusion that the situation and his position could only be salvaged by the imposition of martial law and a return to the authoritarian rule of the centre. In order to maintain his own reputation intact, the President would not take any public part in the coup, but would remain in the Crimea, pretending that he had been kept there either by ill health or – when the public saw through that explanation – by main force on the part of the conspirators. They, meanwhile, would carry out Gorbachov's dirty work, and he would return to the political arena when the deed had been done (Yanayev suggested as much when he said Gorbachov may return to his duties 'when his health was better'). In order to maintain his image as a liberal, Gorbachov would then be able to soften some of the toughest measures introduced by the Emergency Committee, perhaps making a show of sacking some of its members; but he would keep in place the most important consequences of the coup, namely the preservation of the Union, the power of the centre, and the leading role of the President.

This version would give some explanation of why the troops were never ordered to dislodge Yeltsin from the Russian parliament:

bloodshed had to be kept to a minimum, because Gorbachov did not want his fellow plotters or, most of all, himself to be too badly tainted. It would explain why the conspirators ran to Gorbachov when things started to go wrong: they wanted to consult with their boss over what to do next. It would explain why television and radio communications were allowed to remain in place: the plotters did not want to alienate Western countries, because Gorbachov would have need of them when he returned to power; and they actively wanted the West to witness their restraint in not storming Yeltsin's parliament (hence Yanayev's anguished 'Oh no. We didn't expect this!', when he was told of the three deaths on the barricades).

The one thing this version does not explain is why the plotters would go along with a plan that would bring Gorbachov power and glory, but would leave them in the role of hardline usurpers to be castigated by the President when he finally returned from his 'illness'. The answer to that objection, argue the supporters of the conspiracy theory, is that only a few of the plotters were actually in Gorbachov's confidence; the others, who were essentially being exploited by those in the know, thought they really were staging a coup to seize power for themselves. They would be the ones to get fired by Gorbachov when he returned, while the President's confidants would be left in office under the new administration. (Rumour has also abounded in connection with the suicides of three of the plotters: Boris Pugo, Marshal Sergei Akhromeyev, and Nikolai Kruchina, the party's head of organization and finance. One popular theory holds that the men did not commit suicide at all, but were murdered to prevent them revealing the truth about the plot they had entered into, only to be double-crossed.)

This scenario also had the advantage, from Gorbachov's point of view, that if things went wrong (as indeed they did), he would be kept safely away from blame and able to repudiate everything the State Emergency Committee had done. The double-crossed plotters might try to tell the world about Gorbachov's involvement (as Lukyanov did in his remarks to journalists), but nobody would believe them. Everyone would conclude that they were simply trying to divert the blame away from themselves (this was Gorbachov's explanation of Lukyanov's accusations when they were put to him at the Russian parliament session).

Such an explanation accounts for many of the seeming inconsistencies in the behaviour of the State Emergency Committee and of Gorbachov himself. But it fails to explain satisfactorily why the plotters would agree to leave Boris Yeltsin in a position of public influence. To say that they spared the Russian parliament to avoid offending world opinion by the spilling of blood; does not allow for the aim of the supposed conspiracy being ultimately to install a new authoritarian regime, and there was no way that Yeltsin – if left at large – would allow that plan to be carried through. By sparing Yeltsin, the plotters were allowing potentially their most troublesome enemy to continue his fight against them.

The more sophisticated conspiracy theorists explain this inconsistency by adding that Yeltsin himself was part of the plot. The Moscow City Deputy, Boris Kagarlitsky, argued this in an article published after the coup in Western newspapers. But such versions inevitably become so convoluted that they quickly lose credibility. A three-way pact between Gorbachov, Yanayev and Yeltsin would only have been viable if all three had agreed that the ultimate outcome would be a government of national unity involving hardliners, moderates and extreme radicals – a very unlikely set-up. The actual outcome was less than a success for two of the three parties (Yanayev and Gorbachov), with only Yeltsin profiting. To explain this away involves intricate plots of a double-cross by Yeltsin, and the implausible agreement of the other two not to reveal their initial plot.

There is, however, an alternative theory which also involves Gorbachov's participation in the coup, but which supposes very different motives. By the summer of 1991 Gorbachov had made an irrevocable decision to abandon the hardliners and to press ahead with his Union Treaty dismantling the power of the centre. He had also come to the conclusion that growing pressure from the reactionaries would make the implementation of the new power structures virtually impossible. The solution was to remove the conservatives from power, but partly through Gorbachov's own actions in the past, the hardliners had become so deeply entrenched at the highest levels of the leadership that they could not be dug out by any conventional political means. His response was to resort to unconventional means, conniving with the conservatives to stage a coup which Gorbachov firmly believed would fail. The hardliners would subsequently be unmasked for what they were: ambitious usurpers bent on restoring dictatorship, but enjoying no support from the people. The collapse of the coup would thus remove Gorbachov's reactionary opponents at one fell swoop, and leave the way clear for him to follow his chosen political course.

This version also runs up against some of the same objections. Why, for instance, would the plotters agree to play a role which had every chance of leading them to personal disaster? The answer, according to proponents of the theory, is that Gorbachov tricked them into staging their bid for power by promising to join them in their enterprise: when the coup was already under way, he played his master card by backing out of the agreement and leaving Yanayev and the others in the lurch. He would thus have achieved his main purpose, which was to give the hardliners enough rope to hang themselves, and then to stand back and watch them commit political suicide. This version, like the previous one, provides a convincing explanation of the plotters' naive belief that Gorbachov would come to their aid during the coup. It explains their dash to the Crimea to rejoin the man who had put them up to the putsch; it explains their surprise when the President deserted them; and it explains Lukyanov's claims that Gorbachov was 'in the know'. What is more, there is a possible precedent for such behaviour by Gorbachov.

In the days before the January crack-down in the Baltics, Gorbachov had consistently and publicly encouraged decisive action by the hardliners. In December 1990 the Soyuz group of deputies had pressed for military action against the breakaway republics, to be followed by the declaration of a state of emergency across the whole country. Despite the outrageousness of Soyuz's demands, Gorbachov never publicly rejected them, and on 10 January he issued a statement to be read on national television, that explicitly backed the hardliners' suggestions. 'Urgent measures must be adopted,' said the President's address. 'The people are demanding the restoration of constitutional order . . . they are demanding the imposition of presidential rule.' Three days later, troops stormed the Lithuanian TV tower and thirteen unarmed civilians were killed; a similar massacre followed within days in Latvia. From the blatant incitement of December and early January, Gorbachov's rhetoric suddenly changed: now he was in favour of a dialogue and a political solution; he disowned the actions of the army and said he had not ordered them. All the suggestions were that Gorbachov had provoked the Baltic putsch and then watched as domestic and international opprobrium descended on the men who carried it out.

The most outspoken leader of the Soyuz group, Colonel Viktor Alksnis, later gave his version of the January events, claiming that Gorbachov had told the hardliners they could count on his support if they acted boldly in the Baltics. He had given his backing to the self-proclaimed National Salvation Committees in the republics and had indicated he would recognize them as legitimate governments if the military could force out the nationalists who had been elected to power. Alksnis suggested that the putsch was planned as a signal for the imposition of emergency rule throughout the Soviet Union; but, he said, Gorbachov got cold feet. Having set the operation in motion at the behest of the President, the hardliners suddenly found they were not receiving the backing they had been promised. There was no public support from Gorbachov, and the cooperation of the military which had previously been forthcoming was withdrawn.

Alksnis explained the turnaround as a loss of nerve by the President in the face of international pressure, but others suggested a more Machiavellian explanation. Gorbachov, they claimed, had planned it all in advance, with the aim of provoking his hardline opponents into an action which would flush them into the open and lead to their removal from power. The theory is given added credibility by Eduard Shevardnadze's dramatic resignation speech a month earlier. He had spoken of impending dictatorship and had left little doubt in his remarks that he believed Gorbachov was conniving in it.

But if Gorbachov's ultimate goal was indeed to deceive and discredit the hardliners, it did not have the desired effect. Despite the massacres in Lithuania and Latvia, no one was brought to justice and no politicians were removed from their posts. Alksnis and Soyuz continued their agitation for further repression, and even Alfred Rubiks, the hardline Communist who led the Latvian National Salvation Committee, was left in place as the republic's party boss.

According to the conspiracy theorists, the Baltic putsch failed in its immediate aim, but was destined to serve as a rehearsal for the coup in August. Then, in August, it seemed at first that things had worked out better. If Gorbachov had been hoping to unmask his hardline enemies by encouraging them into an unwinnable rebellion, he achieved his purpose. If he intended to put the leading opponents of reform behind bars, he succeeded brilliantly. But if he also meant to consolidate his own position as leader of the country, something had gone badly wrong.

When Gorbachov first returned to Moscow from the Crimea, his behaviour suggested that he did believe his purposes had been served. He seemed to think he could simply step back into the position of power he had previously enjoyed, with the added bonus that the conservative opposition had been destroyed. But he was soon disabused: the real beneficiary of the failed coup was Boris

Yeltsin. It was Yeltsin who had led the resistance to the putsch, and who therefore took the public credit for its defeat. The hatred stirred up by the reactionary forces had caused a huge increase in sympathy for radical reform, and the man who promised radical reform was not Mikhail Gorbachov, but Boris Yeltsin. Gorbachov returned from the Crimea to a political power base that had been drastically undermined, not enhanced, by the coup.

The weakness of this theory, therefore, is that it presupposes a Gorbachov who did not have the intelligence to calculate the outcome of the plot he was entering into. Given the perspicacity he had shown in all his other political dealings, it seems highly unlikely that Gorbachov would not have foreseen Boris Yeltsin's exploitation of the coup, and the real danger that represented. At this point, the conspiracy theorists again return to the suggestion that Yeltsin was originally party to the plot, but reneged on his agreement to share the spoils with Gorbachov and seized his chance of gaining sole power for himself. This would account for Gorbachov's stunned reaction at the Friday session of the Russian parliament when Yeltsin proceeded to humiliate him and undermine his authority.

But the weaknesses of the double- or triple-plot theories have been discussed above, and there is little more than a corpus of inconclusive circumstantial evidence for any of them. Indeed, the whole idea that Gorbachov and/or Yeltsin would gamble their own future and that of their country on a conspiracy with so many uncertainties and variables (what if the coup had succeeded?) makes it seem inherently unlikely. The stakes were so high and the dangers so great that it would have taken extreme irresponsibility on the part of any politician to set such a series of events in motion.

Yet the fact remains that millions of Russians believe Gorbachov had a hand in the August events. He himself added to the atmosphere of intrigue in remarks at the end of the Russian parliament session, when he spoke of the 'scenario planning' he had practised with his closest advisers. This had involved planning for the possibility of a coup, working out who would act in certain ways, and speculating on who would gain from such an event.

In the end, suggestions that Gorbachov consciously connived with the plotters are impossible to prove or disprove. There is no conclusive evidence that he was involved in the conspiracy in the conventional sense of plotting with the coup leaders. But there is no doubt that certain of Gorbachov's own actions did contribute directly to the putsch taking place. Whether he intended to provoke such an outcome when he took those actions, or whether he unwittingly sparked a coup which he did not want to happen, is known only to him. The fact remains that Gorbachov's own behaviour was one of the central factors which made the August putsch inevitable. As described in an earlier chapter, Gorbachov made concerted efforts to appoint leading hardliners to positions of power: these were the men who eventually led the coup against him. But, more than that, the President's violent swings between the politics of reform and reaction undoubtedly led those same men to believe they could and should act in the way they did. In the months before the coup, Gorbachov seemed to be doing everything possible to encourage them to make their move. His behaviour during the January putsch in the Baltics, and the support he gave to the proponents of tough measures, have already been mentioned.

Equally revealing was his reaction to the 'gang of four's' attempt to displace him in June. The campaign to force the Supreme Soviet into transferring Gorbachov's presidential powers to the hardline Prime Minister Valentin Pavlov had the backing of Pugo, Kryuchkov and Yazov. Pavlov had presented their demands to a televized session of the parliament, saying he needed the powers to act decisively over the economy. 'There are times,' he said, 'when decisions have to be taken that have nothing to do with the President, and he should not have any say in them.' As in August, the plotters had chosen to strike while Gorbachov was out of Moscow on vacation; but he did have his supporters in the Supreme Soviet, and they subjected Pavlov's demands to intense questioning. Had Pavlov consulted the President about the request to transfer his powers? Pavlov sheepishly answered that he had not. Did Pavlov have major differences with the President? Pavlov hesitated, smiled, hesitated, and finally said, 'I think you already know that.' According to Gorbachov's aides who were at his holiday villa with him, the President seemed annoyed but not particularly shocked by the news of Pavlov's treachery. 'Look how far they have gone! It is a frontal attack now!' was his response (according to his adviser Georgy Shakhnazarov, who was with Gorbachov at the time).

Even more threatening than Pavlov's public bombast was an address made by Kryuchkov to a closed session of the parliament. With the television cameras switched off, he told the deputies that the transfer of powers was necessary because 'the country is on the brink of disaster'. Quoting from an alleged CIA document of the 1970s, Kryuchkov talked of an American plan to infiltrate the Soviet leadership, which would now be coming to fruition. He implied that certain members of the current administration – clearly the liberals – were in fact CIA plants, and that urgent action was needed to move against them. It was an undisguised attempt to subvert the Soviet administration, a semi-constitutional coup, which failed only because Ivan Laptev, the deputy speaker who was chairing the crucial session, refused to put Pavlov's demands to a vote. (Had it been the usual chairman, Anatoly Lukyanov, the move might easily have succeeded.)

When Gorbachov returned to Moscow, he might have been expected to remove from power the men who had challenged his authority, but he did not. Ivan Laptev said Gorbachov took Pavlov, Yazov, Kryuchkov and Pugo into a back room of the parliament and subjected them to a fierce verbal assault. The four of them 'looked embarrassed and tried to change the subject', said Laptev, but Gorbachov kept up his attack. In public, however, the President's only comment on the affair was to say, 'We have no differences with comrade Pavlov.' According to Georgy Shakhnazarov, Gorbachov believed that his henchmen might complain and cause trouble, but would never move to oust him because they were totally dependent on his leadership.

Gorbachov's failure to punish the hardliners in June may have been due to over-confidence, weakness or deliberate subterfuge. Whatever the reason, his ineffectual reaction to their plotting seems to have convinced them that further attempts to seize power were not going to result in any drastic retribution against them.

It seems impossible that Gorbachov actively conspired with the plotters; there is too much evidence to the contrary to accept any of the conspiracy theories so far advanced. But, whether by conscious effort or by neglect, Gorbachov's own actions undoubtedly contributed to the coup which transformed the Soviet Union.

10

'A Different World':
What Now?

When Mikhail Gorbachov returned to Moscow in the early hours of 22 August, he said he felt as though he were returning to 'a different world'. So much had changed in the three days he had been detained in the Crimea, so many fundamental elements of Soviet life had been swept away, that he at first had difficulty in accepting the extent of those changes. He fought against some of them. And in the following weeks and months he resembled a Soviet King Canute unable to reverse the tide of history which had swept across his country and sent its currents throughout the world.

Gorbachov initially talked of pressing ahead with his plans for the Union Treaty, and his only public recognition of the new political balance in the country was an announcement that he would now work closely with the 'other democratic forces', from whom he would 'never again' allow himself to be separated, and in particular with Boris Yeltsin. It took him several days to realize that his power base had been destroyed and that ultimate influence in the Soviet Union had passed to Yeltsin and the leaders of the republics.

But although Gorbachov's slide from power was greatly accelerated in the aftermath of the August coup, it was a process which had already begun months previously. The Union Treaty itself provided for the transfer of much power to the republics; and the logic of Gorbachov's own reforms seemed to point to him eventually being squeezed out of office.

In June 1991 the acerbic Polish Solidarity activist, Adam Michnik, had given me his uncompromising assessment of the dilemma facing Gorbachov

> There's an argument going on about whether Gorby is a democrat at heart, or not. I'm not interested in this. That may be of interest

to his wife. All I'm interested in are the practical consequences. . . .
Gorby has reached a turning point. He has to take a decision
that he and the Communists will first share power and then
– as the result of elections – give it up. That's the essential
dilemma. I wish Gorby enough courage to understand that there
is no other way out for Russia. Any other path will lead to
civil war.

Michnik was perhaps dramatizing, but by the summer of 1991 it was
undeniable that Gorbachov and the Communist party would soon
have to accept the ultimate conclusion of the democratic process he
had initiated: namely that free elections were now a necessity, and
that neither the party nor the President would win.

A few weeks before the August coup, when I put that point
to Anatoly Lukyanov, his response reflected the leadership's acute
awareness of the historical processes which meant their days in power
were numbered: 'We have made the changes, so now democracy
must operate. Let there be multi-candidate elections according to
the rules. . . .I don't see this as a tragedy. Both Mr Gorbachov and
I are looking to the long term . . . our task has been so huge, and
we have changed society so much, that we could say we have done
our bit. I don't know any other politician who could do the same.'
Lukyanov, of course, was dissembling when he claimed he was ready
to step down from power: even at the time he was talking, he was
planning to use the coup as a means of holding onto office despite
the wishes of the people. But his remarks confirmed that the changes
which took place so rapidly after the August putsch were beginning
to take shape in the months leading up to it. The Communists and
Gorbachov were already losing their grip on power, and they were
aware of it. They would almost certainly have been removed from
office in the medium term (elections were tentatively scheduled for
spring 1992). The coup merely had the effect of making everything
happen with breathtaking speed.

Gorbachov's initial attempts to avert the disintegration of the
Communist party when he returned from the Crimea were a
reflection of his desire to slow down the processes which had
been thrown into overdrive by the August events. He knew that
the party was his only remaining power base: the people were behind
Boris Yeltsin, and the accelerating changes in the political balance
were taking control of the economic, military and logistical levers
of power away from the centre and into the hands of the republics.
Gorbachov's only hope of retaining overall influence was to preserve
the structures of the party *apparat* which had run Soviet society for

decades and which would still remain answerable to him. It was an irony that the man who in February 1991 had deliberately weakened the influence of the party was now looking to it to rescue his tenuous claims to power.

In the end, of course, it was all academic. On 22 August Gorbachov was still fighting for the party, defending the Central Committee and calling on the democrats to avoid a 'witch hunt' against its members. But by 23 August he had caved in. Under relentless pressure from Boris Yeltsin (which was, in effect, the public formulation of the wishes of the Russian people), he signed the party's death warrant. Had he broken with Communism before the coup, Gorbachov might have regained his old prestige and put himself back in the vanguard of political change. Even a clear rejection of a treacherous party as soon as he returned from the Crimea might still have saved him. But he had prevaricated and revealed his personal attachment to a movement which the people now hated. His ultimate banning of the party brought him little credit: it made him look like a man swept along by events and by Boris Yeltsin. When Eduard Shevardnadze heard the news of Gorbachov's decree, he sighed, 'I told him he should have done that long ago.'

What Gorbachov's announcement did do, though, was to unleash a popular desire for vengeance against the party which had ruled with ruthless tenacity for seven decades. On the streets, that vengeance took the form of the destruction of statues and symbols. But at the same time, the party's structures were being methodically closed down and its property confiscated by the forces of Boris Yeltsin's Russian republic. Following the lead of Gavriil Popov, who had begun the sealing of Moscow party headquarters even before Gorbachov's decree, police were despatched to local offices and Communist cells in factories and enterprises all over the country. Yeltsin's investigators demanded and received access to the files of the KGB: their immediate aim was to establish the organization's complicity in the coup, but the operation would also reveal records of the countless crimes committed by the Communists' security police and add to the growing atmosphere of hatred.

In the Proletarsky region of Moscow, we filmed one of Yeltsin's envoys as he took possession of the party headquarters. The demoralized former occupants offered no resistance, and the investigators rifled through their desks and filing cabinets, eagerly seizing any papers which aroused their suspicion. Yeltsin's men were keen to recount how they were uncovering the secrets of a system which had thrived on covert dealings: 'There are documents here which have to be seized urgently. Just yesterday we confiscated two secret circulars from the party's top leadership, and they are now being investigated for use as evidence . . . now here they've got a special secret department, and that means they've got something to hide.'

Documents brought back from party locales confirmed suspicions that the Central Committee had been active during the coup. In a desperate attempt to clear themselves, the Committee secretariat issued a statememt protesting their innocence: 'We condemn the use of temporary emergency measures to install an authoritarian regime, the creation of unconstitutional organs of power, and the attempt to use force. . . . The Secretariat reaffirms its commitment to the course of democratic renewal in Soviet society.' Unfortunately for the Central Committee, their 'protest' against the coup came long after the coup was over, and was too late to save them. *Pravda* also tried to redeem itself with a front-page announcement claiming that it opposed the coup: 'In these troubled days, when our country is living through one of the most critical periods of its history, the editorial board of *Pravda* will strive to report all events with objectivity, and will remain always faithful to the course of democratic renewal which began in April 1985.' Objectivity, however, had been sorely lacking when the newspaper printed Yanayev's propaganda; and the issue in which the lame attempt at self-justification appeared (Friday, 23 August) was the last before Boris Yeltsin ordered *Pravda*'s suspension and the replacement of its staff.

Even the KGB had a go at excusing itself in a statement issued the same day: 'Members of the KGB had nothing to do with the illegal acts of that group of adventurists. The KGB is deeply afflicted by the fact that its honour has been besmirched by the involvement of the chairman of the KGB in the activities of the so-called State Emergency Committee.'

The protestations of innocence were, of course, too late. All the organs of the party had been tainted by the coup, and even those which had taken no direct role in it were unable to escape the wrath of the people. The anti-Communist witch hunt that Gorbachov had vainly tried to prevent was in full swing. The Supreme Soviet endorsed Gorbachov's dismissal of the entire government and then debated its own guilt in the coup, amid calls for the parliament to disband itself as a sign of repentance. Its deputy speaker, the liberal Ivan Laptev, castigated the deputies: 'We have to pay the penalty for our three days of silence during the coup. I feel acute shame that a handful of political adventurists flouted all democratic norms, and we pretended it was not our concern.' The KGB leadership was purged and the organization put into the hands of the liberal Vadim Bakatin: his first act was to propose the immediate banning of the KGB. And Yevgeny Shaposhnikov, the genial general who opposed the use of the army during the 'coup, was appointed Defence Minister to replace the discredited Yazov.

The loosening of decades of repression resulted in virulent anti-Communist attacks in the chamber of the Supreme Soviet, with individual members of the party vainly trying to defend themselves. Central Committee spokesman Aleksandr Dzasokhov tried to calm the deputies who were baying for blood: 'The Communist party as an organization,' he protested, 'had nothing to do with the coup. We were against extremism . . . but now there is moral terror, and even physical terror, being unleashed against millions of innocent people.' A tearful Valentin Falin, the former ambassador to West Germany and a long-time Central Committee *apparatchik*, told the chamber how he too had become a target of the anti-Communist campaign: 'Comrades, while I was speaking to you here yesterday, they came to search my flat. My wife was told that if she didn't open up, they would break down the door . . . [sobs] . . . But why are they doing this, comrades? I have not been accused of any crime. . . .' The Communist hardliners were getting some of the medicine they had meted out for seven decades, and they did not like the taste.

On Russian television, a telephone number was displayed every evening for citizens who wanted to inform on neighbours who had supported the coup. For many, the anti-Communist purges were becoming distastefully reminiscent of the Stalinist tactics used in the 1930s.

One of the key targets of the growing hatred was Anatoly Lukyanov, the mastermind behind the putsch. He was allowed to stay free for several days after the coup: he had not publicly declared his membership of the State Emergency Committee, and Gorbachov seemed reluctant to act against his old comrade. Lukyanov was thus able to defend himself at the Supreme Soviet, denying that he had betrayed his mentor: 'I have to say, looking you straight in the eyes, that I was not and could not be a conspirator . . . still less the ideological inspiration behind the whole conspiracy as they have tried to state here. I fully accept the President's criticism. There was disarray and confusion, ignorance of the true situation, but I have to say that I did not betray anyone.'

But the attacks were taking their toll. Lukyanov looked increasingly haggard and wild-eyed as he stumbled round the corridors of parliament. His last card was to invoke the dangerous consequences for the country that the attacks on Communists and the removal of the party's unifying structures throughout the land were beginning to have: 'The Union is breaking up, the structures of power destroyed and people discredited.If we continue this witch hunt, an even worse crisis awaits us. We must not allow that to happen.' But even the threat of a post-Communist deluge could not save Lukyanov. On 29 August the State Prosecutor, Nikolai Trubin, addressed the Supreme Soviet and asked it to lift the protection of parliamentary immunity from its former speaker. The overwhelming vote meant Lukyanov's arrest and incarceration on charges of capital treason. But such was the fury with which the Communists were being driven from power that the man who had just arrested Lukyanov went on in the next breath to tender his own resignation! Trubin explained that he was taking responsibility for his department's behaviour during the coup and his departure was greeted with loud applause. It was Trubin who had infuriated the liberals with his cynical report on the Baltic massacres, in which he concluded that the troops had killed no one and that it was the separatists who fired on the army.

Some of the plotters, though, had escaped the grasp of earthly justice. Marshal Sergei Akhromeyev's suicide made him the third (along with Boris Pugo and Nikolai Kruchina) to die by his own hand. In his note of farewell, he said he had backed the coup to protect the socialist achievements he had fought for all his life; when the takeover failed, he hanged himself. At his funeral, which took place with military honours, the mourners were bitter at the treatment Akhromeyev had received, blaming those who were stirring up anti-Communist hysteria for causing his death.

The end of the party's influence also brought the end of its institutions. The hardline television news programme, *Vremya*, was taken off the air after twenty-three years, to be replaced by a new programme whose presenters promised in their first bulletin to do away with the Communists' brand of news management and replace it with independent, objective reporting. *Pravda* eventually reappeared, but it too had been transformed. No longer the organ of the (disbanded) Central Committee, it had lost its traditional subtitle and its front-page motto of 'Workers of the world unite'.

Now, with a completely new editorial team, it was simply called a 'general political newspaper'.

The new media freedoms brought a storm of attacks on the party, with new 'Communist scandals' being reported every day. Some, like the tale of confiscated Central Committee documents which showed party donations of three billion roubles to Saddam Hussein, were never proved, but they nonetheless added to the atmosphere of post-Communist gloating and vengeance.

The end of Communist power was formally marked by a bizarre ceremony in Gorky Park, when the radical mayor of Moscow, Gavriil Popov, officially inaugurated what was referred to as an 'open-air museum of social history'. The museum consisted of all the Communist statues which had been removed from sites in Moscow and had now been declared historic relics. In a show of informality which the prone Dzerzhinskys, Serovs and Lenins would have been unlikely to appreciate, their deposed effigies were piled up on the grass for the crowds to come and treat as they liked. Popov drew the moral, speaking of the museum as a symbolic exhibit to show the people that one era of history had ended, leaving them free to begin the construction of a new age.

The excision of Communism from the fabric of Soviet society was an exhilarating process for those who took an active part in it; but it created far-reaching problems for the normal functioning of the state. Banning the CPSU was not like banning a political party in a Western democracy. The movement was not just a party: over seventy years it had in many respects become the state. When it disappeared, virtually overnight, it left a yawning void in all areas of Soviet existence. Gorbachov's spokesman Vitaly Ignatenko summed up what the disappearance of Communism meant for a nation born and bred in its arms

> You have to imagine a society whose resources have been allocated and whose needs have been supplied for decades by the party. If a young man wanted to have a career, he had to be a member of the party. Everything was connected with the party. I even remember a poem published by a young girl in the Communist youth newspaper. It said: 'Winter has gone, Summer has come, Thanks be to the party.' It sounds naive and funny today. But in the context of those days, it really wasn't a childish matter. We had to thank the party for everything. . . .And all of a sudden, to become aware that you can choose your own future, build your own life, without having to be beholden to the party. . . .

For generations of Soviets, the party had been a religion; and in August 1991 they discovered that God was dead.

In political terms, the collapse of Communism left a power vacuum which threatened to lead to chaos. The Soviet Union had been a one-party state for seventy-four years; other political movements had only been allowed to operate since February 1991, and they were still in their earliest infancy. The initial enthusiasm for party politics after the long Communist monopoly meant that a plethora of half-formed groups registered their existence, but very few of them had a strong enough organization or following to survive in the political arena. Eduard Shevardnadze's Movement for Democratic Reforms looked capable of making a certain impact: it attracted reformers like Gavriil Popov, Aleksandr Yakovlev and the liberal economist Pavel Bunich. But the party had not even held its founding congress by the time the coup took place (it was officially formed only at the end of September), and Shevardnadze himself admitted that it would have a hard time opposing former Communists who had remained active despite their party's demise: 'We are in the midst of economic and, to some degree, political chaos. We must help those reformers who gained power after the coup to pull our country out of this crisis.'

At the party's opening conference, Gavriil Popov added to earlier warnings by Shevardnadze and others that another hardline attempt to seize power could not yet be ruled out: 'In August, we defeated fools. But now they are finding smarter leaders.' The possible threat of another coup added to the democrats' urgent efforts to unite their forces. Pavel Bunich warned of the dangers of allowing liberal forces to divide their strength by splitting into too many parties: 'The Communists are still strong and we would be naive to think they have been swept from the historical arena. Together we can be stronger than they are; but if we divide, then they will be the stronger.'

Other radical parties joined the call for a united movement, including Yeltsin's Democratic Russia party, the Ecological Movement and Aleksandr Rutskoi's Democratic Communists of Russia (which retained its old name pending a collective decision on a new one). But the democrats had had no experience of political organization and they were starting life at an overwhelming disadvantage. In themselves, they would not be enough to fill the vacuum left by the Communists.

Before the coup, the intention had been to allow new parties to arise naturally on the political scene and eventually (it was promised) challenge the CPSU for supremacy. That process had, however, scarcely begun. The Communist monopoly had not been replaced by multi-party democracy; instead, a semi-feudal system of powerful barons had develped, each jostling for the right to issue decrees and to rule his fiefdom without the interference of the tsar in Moscow. The barons were the presidents of the republics, most powerful of whom was Boris Yeltsin, and the current tsar was Mikhail Gorbachov. As well as aspiring to absolute power in his Russian fiefdom, Yeltsin had led the ideological fight against Communism, and it was he – not any of the fledgling parties – who was the first to rush into the post-Communist power vacuum.

He seized on the chaos and disruption caused by the coup to cement his victory in the 'war of laws' he had been fighting against Gorbachov. As president of Russia, Yeltsin had long argued that Russian law must take precedence on the territory of his republic; but Gorbachov, as Soviet President, had ruled that Russian legislation remain subordinate to that of the central Soviet authorities. The clash had reached critical proportions in 1990, when both men had voted themselves the power to rule by presidential decree, and the population did not know which version of the law they were supposed to obey. (When Gorbachov imposed a tax on fur coats and certain other items, for instance, Yeltsin immediately responded by banning the tax in Russia.)

Under the conditions of the coup, with Gorbachov removed from the political scene and with chaos threatening, Yeltsin profited from the occasion to issue a series of emergency decrees. Most of these were straightforward anti-putsch measures, overturning the decrees of the State Emergency Committee or directing local officials to oppose the conspirators, but towards the end of the coup period, Yeltsin was emboldened to issue directives which usurped the powers of the Soviet President. He began to appoint his own candidates to take charge of central government ministries, jobs which should have been decided by Gorbachov; and he moved to take control of economic functions which should have belonged to the central authorities.

Yeltsin's argument was always that Gorbachov was a prisoner and that someone had to act decisively in his absence. But he kept up his stream of high-handed decrees even after Gorbachov had returned to Moscow. In the new conditions of political flux, where many forces were jockeying for power, this was a clear attempt to see how far he could push Gorbachov: he wanted to exploit Gorbachov's natural gratitude to him for the role Russia had played in defeating the coup, and to use this to establish his own supremacy in the legislative process.

At first it worked well for Yeltsin, with Gorbachov agreeing to endorse retroactively all the decrees he had passed during the time of the coup. (Yeltsin used this to dramatic effect during the Friday session of the Russian parliament, when he issued his startling order to ban the Communist Party of Russia.) But then Yeltsin pushed his luck too far: on the morning of 28 August, he announced a new decree which would bring the Soviet Central Bank under the control of his Russian authorities. That same evening, it was announced that the decree had been annulled and the Bank was back under Gorbachov's control. The Soviet President had fought back and had, at least temporarily, stemmed the tide of Yeltsin's push for unlimited power.

The rivalry between the two men continued, however, and the final power balance was decidedly in the favour of Boris Yeltsin. He persuaded Gorbachov to accept his closest allies in positions of the highest influence in the Soviet government, and Ivan Silayev, Yeltsin's loyal lieutenant, was given the position of acting Prime Minister, with special powers to run the Soviet economy, while Grigory Yavlinsky, the radical economist who co-authored Yeltsin's favoured 500 day economic programme, was appointed Deputy Prime Minister, seemingly guaranteeing the triumph of his liberal market ideas. Silayev and Yavlinsky quickly called together economics ministers from all fifteen republics to discuss the coordination of their economies after the disintegration of the Soviet Union. The fact that even separatist republics like the Baltics sent representatives reflected the trust the Russian leadership was held in, compared to Gorbachov, who had long failed to bring all the republics together for discussions on any topic. Silayev's diplomacy would stand Yeltsin in good stead when it came to negotiating a post-USSR settlement for the country's future structure.

Having ceded much of his authority to Yeltsin and having seen the Russian leader install his own men in positions of power, Gorbachov suffered further set-backs. In an effort to re-establish his standing among the democrats, he publicly asked leading radicals like Eduard Shevardnadze, Aleksandr Yakovlev and Gavriil Popov to join his new team of close advisers. But most of them had been on Gorbachov's team in the past, and most had been discarded by the President when he swung towards the hardliners in the winter of 1990. Perhaps disillusioned with Gorbachov's unreliability, or perhaps in a fit of pique at not being offered the Foreign Minister's job, Shevardnadze publicly humiliated his old boss by turning the offer down. Yakovlev, Popov and the others followed suit; and on the following day, Askar Akayev, the liberal president of Kirgizia, completed Gorbachov's misery by turning down his offer of the Soviet deputy presidency.

With the collapse of the Communist party, and with Yeltsin's aggressive quest for influence, Gorbachov had been left friendless and seemingly marginalized in the new balance of power in the country. The significance of the post of Soviet President had been much reduced by the disintegration of the Union and the transfer of power to the republics. Even the areas which did remain in the competence of the centre were being taken over by Yeltsin's own nominees in the Soviet government. The only crumb of comfort was the pledge by Russian Vice-President Aleksandr Rutskoi that he and Yeltsin would back Gorbachov in a future election for the Soviet presidency: with Gorbachov already widely seen as Yeltsin's puppet, it was clearly an arrangement that the Russian leader wanted to keep in place for his own purposes.

The party structures which had long bound the Soviet Union together, with their ubiquitous control of social, administrative, economic and political functions throughout the country, had gone. The men who once ran them had been fired; no Communist official had been left in existence. The duties once fulfilled by the party, however, still had to be carried out; and the immediate solution was to transfer the party's old responsibilities (along with its property and resources) to the state bodies which had existed in parallel with the Communist structures and had previously been dominated by them. These state bodies were, in the first instance, the local and town councils, known as Soviets.

Soviets had existed since the revolution and had always been elected bodies. In the old days, of course, only Communists could stand for election but since Gorbachov introduced the idea of multi-candidate (but not multi-party) elections in 1989, opposition radicals had begun to be elected. In the big cities like Moscow and Leningrad, the democrats were in the majority, because the politically aware urban populations had voted en masse for liberal candidates in the spring elections of 1990. In the backward rural areas, however, it was the Communists who won the majority of seats; and even though these men and women had been sacked from their party posts, they still retained their positions in the Soviets. Thus, in many places the transfer of responsibility from the party structures to the elected state bodies did not give power to the democrats, but handed it back to the Communists in a different guise. Yeltsin knew the old-guard politicians running the Soviets in the countryside would be less than enthusiastic to implement the radical legislation he was passing; and it was too long to wait for the next elections to remove them from power. He expected the former Communists to begin a campaign of deliberate sabotage, so in order to ensure his decrees were carried out, he began to despatch his own men from Moscow to oversee their activities.

The concept of government inspectors was an old one in Russia. The tsars had had their own network of envoys who were constantly travelling around the country, trying to ensure that the tsar's will was being done. The government inspector was a powerful man. Nikolai Gogol's play of the same name depicts the fear that a visit by one of them could strike into the hearts of local officials, and Boris Yeltsin was hoping to produce the same effect.

In fact, Yeltsin's envoys could do little to uproot the old Communists who remained in place in the Soviets. What they did do, though, was to provide a safety net for Yeltsin, reporting back on resistance to his policies and trying to make a potentially hostile bureaucracy work for the benefit of the reformist politicians in the Russian White House. Most of all, they were able to act as Yeltsin's eyes and ears, seeking out the first signs of revolt among the former Communists, and – Yeltsin hoped – giving him early warning of any moves towards another coup.

The new arrangements for the administration of power were clearly unsatisfactory and open to abuse. They could be no more than a makeshift replacement for what went before; the sudden collapse of the Communist structures had been a shattering blow to the Soviet state and the task of restoring political equilibrium was immense. The threat of a Communist resurgence could not be discounted, and the continuing chaos in the structures of power was being exacerbated by the other momentous consequence of the August coup: the headlong disintegration of the Soviet Union.

As seen in earlier chapters, the momentum for the break-up of the USSR had been increasing well before the coup. After years of prevarication and opposition, Gorbachov had signalled his recognition of this process by accepting the provisions of the draft Union Treaty, which met some of the republic's demands for greater autonomy, but still attempted to maintain significant influence for the centre and the Soviet President. The coup changed all that in a trice.

With the banning of the Communist party, the country's main unifying force disappeared. The CPSU's guiding principle had always been 'democratic centralism', a system under which the regions delegated power to the centre, and the centre's decisions were final. Thus, the rulings of the party authorities were binding for the whole Soviet Union and acted as a guarantee of uniformity in a state where ethnic, territorial and historic diversity would otherwise have resulted in political schisms. The other two traditional guarantors of unity, the army and the KGB, had shown in August that they were either incapable or unwilling to fulfil that role. So when the party collapsed and the pro-autonomy Boris Yeltsin took on the mantle of power, the prospect of an early break-up of the Union came a step closer.

Seizing their chance, one republic after the other declared their independence from Moscow. The Baltics, Armenia and Georgia had already done so, but on 24 August they were joined by the Ukraine, the most powerful of all the republics after Russia itself. The formerly quiescent Byelorussia was next, on 25 August; and then Moldova on the 26th; Azerbaijan on the 30th; and even the loyal central Asians of Uzbekistan and Kirgizia had gone by the end of the month. For some of the republics, declaring independence was mainly a tactical move. The smaller ones knew they could not survive on their own, and even the mighty Ukraine had a population which was divided on the issue of independence. The internal politics in Azerbaijan were so complex that it was hard to work out who wanted what. But with the USSR in its death throes, and with a new structure seemingly about to emerge, they all felt that staking their claim to independence would secure their negotiating position when the new relationship between the republics was worked out.

The shape of the new structures to replace the old Soviet Union was the subject of heated debate both in the parliaments and on the streets. Several republics, notably the Baltics and Georgia, wanted nothing to do with their former partners in the USSR, except for trading and economic relations. Many Moldovans were pressing for union with their ethnic and linguistic brothers in Roumania. But the weaker republics, those which had been most dependent on the Soviet economy, and those which had been most loyal to Moscow, were looking for the preservation of considerably greater ties. Russia, the dominant party in any discussion about the future, was for the moment keeping its own counsel.

If the discussions on the future of the Union had been passionate before the coup, they were now becoming frenetic. Mikhail Gorbachov showed the extent of his confusion with two speeches on consecutive days which flatly contradicted each other. In the first, on 26 August, he made a seemingly unconditional offer of immediate talks with any republic wishing to leave the Union. He made no mention of the complex and almost unmeetable set of restrictions he had previously placed in the way of secession, and seemed to have bowed to the avalanche of support for Boris Yeltsin's laissez-faire approach. But on the following day, he suddenly announced that he remained committed to preserving the Union, and would resign if he failed to do so.

The threat of resignation from an unpopular and marginalized Soviet President no longer carried the force it did when he had used it in the past; but it showed that Gorbachov was still harbouring plans for some sort of federation between his former subjects, involving at the very least binding economic if not political ties. On the same day as his pro-Union speech he gave some indication of what he had in mind, by inviting six republics to talks in the Kremlin at which he won their agreement to remain linked in an economic union. Gorbachov had come back from the Crimea still talking about the need to press ahead with his Union Treaty: now he had seemingly accepted that the Treaty would never be signed, at least not in anything like its original form.

All the talking and debating, however, soon looked like being overtaken by events on the streets. Already, the substantial Russian-speaking minority in Moldova had staged demonstrations to protest against the republic's independence declaration. A few weeks later, the hardline Communists in Tajikistan were to attempt a rear-guard action against the disbanding of their party and the break-up of the Union. But the most threatening moment came on 27 August, when Boris Yeltsin's mighty Russian republic finally showed its hand. Covering three-quarters of the Soviet Union's land mass, with more than half the population and the vast bulk of the country's natural resources, Russia's opinion was always going to be decisive. Because Yeltsin had consistently supported the right of republics to secede, most had assumed that he would not now make difficulties, but in parliament that afternoon, one of Yeltsin's aides dropped a bombshell: if republics bordering on Russia opted for independence, he said, then Russia would reserve the right to redraw their common frontiers. The reason given was that large areas of other republics were populated by mainly Russian communities, and the redefinition of borders 'may be necessary' to bring these back under Russian control.

The reaction from the other republics – and especially from Kazakhstan and the Ukraine, which were the two most likely to be affected by any territorial claims – was immediate and outraged. President Nursultan Nazarbayev of Kazakhstan predicted that if Yeltsin tried to redraw republican frontiers, there would be war; and the Ukrainians said there would be a bloody disintegration reminiscent of Yugoslavia if Russia's demands were not withdrawn. Gorbachov – left with only a minor role, as the newly independent republics ignored the centre and argued among themselves – tried to play the thankless part of referee. 'All the statements and decisions and speeches on this issue from the Russian leadership,' he told the parliament, 'are part of a particular polemic, and I don't believe this is a final position. It is clear that we are not going to review any borders.' Whatever Gorbachov might say, however, it was Russia which was calling the shots, and for the first time the prospect of violence as the empire dissolved was a real threat.

There were several reasons behind Yeltsin's ultimatum. He had altered his position on independence quite sharply since ascending to the heights of power. In his former role as critical opposition to Gorbachov and the Communists, it had been in his interests to support secessionist republics; it was a weapon he had used to try to destabilize the Kremlin power structures against which he was struggling. But since he himself had come to power, he had moved much closer to Gorbachov's position of wanting to see the Union survive in some form. This was important to Russia from an economic point of view; and since Yeltsin was now virtually carving up power with Gorbachov as his junior partner, it was in his interests to avoid any major upheavals which could jeopardize that arrangement. While Yeltsin could accept the departure of the Baltics (indeed, he actively supported them in their struggles in January and remained committed to their independence), he seems to have been alarmed by the Ukraine's move to break away. Besides economics, he may well have had in mind the growing pressure for independence from minorities within his own Russian republic: with ethnic Tatars and others seeking separation from Russia, he may have felt that to acquiesce in the republics' drive for secession would undermine his authority in opposing separatism on his own territory.

Whatever the reasons for it, Russia's attempt at intimidation sparked great anxiety. The republics began to fear that the domination of the Communists might be replaced by the domination of an overbearing Russia. Leonid Kravchuk, the Ukrainian President, said the suggestion of redrawing borders had sent reverberations around the whole country: 'A typical imperialist way of thinking has come into play . . . that is, that Russia is still an empire and the rest should submit to it, with no right to choose for themselves.' Those republics which felt themselves threatened by Russia – including the Ukraine – began to form their own national guards to protect their territory and independence, and the frightening prospect of civil war on a scale unseen in the country's history raised its head.

In the face of such a potential nightmare, Russia softened its rhetoric. There had always been some suspicion that the borders ultimatum was a negotiating ploy by Yeltsin, in the hope of scaring the others into accepting his terms for a future confederal structure binding the former republics. This seemed to be borne out when the Russian Vice-President, Aleksandr Rutskoi, was despatched on a peace mission first to the Ukraine and then to Kazakhstan. In the Ukrainian capital, Kiev, his delegation was given a rowdy and hostile reception, and the rest of the country waited anxiously for the result of talks which would determine whether the old Soviet Union was to end its days peacefully or in violence.

In the end, good sense prevailed and Russia agreed to sign an accord with the Ukraine, guaranteeing each other's borders. In return, the Ukraine accepted an economic and military cooperation accord, which gave Yeltsin the assurances he wanted about future trading ties. With Russia relying on Ukrainian food products for much of its supplies, this ultimately seemed to be what Yeltsin had been angling for in the first place. A nascent economic war, with Russia withholding some gas supplies to the Ukraine, and Kiev retaliating by blocking food deliveries, had been avoided for the moment at least. Rutskoi then flew on to Kazakhstan, where the same satisfactory conclusion was reached.

With the old guarantees of central control removed, the prospect of a free for all, as the republics tried to grab what they could from the disintegrating empire, had been a real possibility. Economic quarrels, such as that threatened between Russia and the Ukraine, were the most likely grounds for conflict between the newly independent

states, and the inter-republican accords became a symbol of hope
that such conflict might be avoided.

The accords, though, were direct agreements between the leaders
of individual republics and seemed to cut out the possibility of any
role for the centre or for the Soviet President. It was a point made
forcefully by Leningrad mayor, Anatoly Sobchak: 'We now need
urgently to agree on the future principles of our co-existence.
They could be like the British Commonwealth, like the European
Community, or like a free economic confederation. But Gorbachov
is the President: he must resolve these questions or resign.'

A week after Rutskoi's talks in Kiev, Gorbachov made a last
attempt to secure his influence in the post-Soviet future. At a
day-long meeting in the Kremlin, he and Yeltsin persuaded ten
of the fifteen republican presidents to initial a blueprint for a new
power structure. The objective was to transfer power from the
centre to the republics, without provoking the collapse of the whole
country. Gorbachov accepted that the former republics had now
become sovereign states, free to run their own affairs (the Baltics'
de facto independence was formally recognized by the Congress of
People's Deputies); and they in return agreed to entrust responsibility
for security and military matters to an interim Council of State, made
up of representatives from the ten republics.

A similar Inter-Republican Economic Committee would coordi-
nate economic interests. The benefits consisted of continued participation in the collective trading structures of the old Union and
the collective defence of external borders. Those republics which
refused to take part (notably the Baltics) were to be penalized by
having to pay international, not rouble, prices for Russian gas
and other commodities. Those which did come on board were
promised that the new structures defining the future shape of the
state would reconcile their real independence with the preservation of
the economic ties which had developed between them over decades.
The agreement was modest enough, but it did at least set some
guidelines for the future shape of a tentatively named Union of
Sovereign States, and it raised expectations that a bloody Yugoslav
style disintegration might be avoided.

The fact remained, however, that the move towards separatism
contained the seeds of possible future conflict. None of the newly
independent republics was ethnically homogeneous and the precon-
ditions for national strife were all there. Several republics followed
the lead of the Ukraine in forming their own national guards: the

hundreds of tanks and guns previously controlled by the Soviet army were in danger of becoming the playthings of unstable regimes. Deep-rooted regional hatreds, like that caused by the treatment of Georgia's minorities by the dictatorial nationalist president Zviad Gamsakhurdia; or like that between Armenia and Azerbaijan over the disputed territory of Nagorno Karabakh, could never be removed by agreements on a piece of paper. In the Karabakh conflict, the new post-Communist Union managed a provisional victory, with Boris Yeltsin using his political credit to secure a basic ceasefire accord. Such success would have been unthinkable under the old Kremlin authorities, but it was no guarantee that other issues could be settled in the same way.

As well as the fundamental changes which it wrought in the internal political structure of the Soviet Union, the coup had an electrifying effect on relations with the rest of the world. The international reaction to the August events was split along almost predictable lines. Fidel Castro's orthodox Communists in Cuba welcomed Yanayev's takeover immediately, presumably believing it signalled a return to the true path of Marxism-Leninism. As subsequent events were to prove, it was a somewhat over-hasty reaction which rebounded against the Cubans when the former masters of the Kremlin were restored. The Iraqis too hailed the coup: they had felt betrayed by the support their former ally Gorbachov had given to the Americans in the Gulf War, and they greeted his downfall with undisguised *schadenfreude*.

The initial response of the Western democracies was one of caution. Several considerations were at work as far as Washington, London and the others were concerned. They were, undeniably, in the debt of Gorbachov: he had been the prime mover in ending the cold war; he had agreed to massive money-saving arms cuts; he had taken the heat out of regional conflicts like those in Afghanistan, Angola and south-east Asia; and he had brought the beginnings of democracy to the second superpower. Less than a year earlier, the world had recognized this by awarding him the Nobel peace prize.

But in the first hours after the military takeover, considerations other than gratitude were creeping into the Western leaders' thoughts. On the morning of Monday, 19 August, Gorbachov was looking very much like yesterday's man, and George Bush – with the pragmatism of a professional politician – was thinking that he might soon be having to work with Gennady Yanayev. Hence in his first reaction, he charitably described Yanayev as 'a man with a certain commitment to reform'. By the Monday evening, though, Bush had received information from the CIA that the coup was looking less than secure, and the White House's position suddenly hardened against Yanayev. 'We must avoid in every possible way,' said a presidential statement, 'actions which would lend legitimacy or support to this coup effort.'

The switch in the US position was due largely to the resistance that Boris Yeltsin and his followers were offering to the putsch. Yeltsin had telephoned Bush from inside his besieged parliament and appealed to the Americans to take a tougher line against the Yanayev regime. Bush accepted this advice, but when American support was switched away from Yanayev it was given not so much to Yeltsin but to the absent Gorbachov. On 20 August Bush announced: 'We will continue to try to stand with Mr Gorbachov, as Yeltsin is trying to do.' He said the policy of supporting Gorbachov 'remains the best hope for democracy and reform'; and when the coup collapsed, Bush rather hopefully announced that Gorbachov was 'back fulfilling his duties and calling the shots'. When it was pointed out to him, as late as 22 August, that Yeltsin might have been the real hero of the coup, Bush was still unwilling to give credit where credit was due: 'This jumping on Gorbachov, I'm just not going to be a part of it. . . . Let's recognize that not only is eastern Europe free, Germany reunited and troops moving back, but that he launched a very ambitious programme on perestroika and glasnost.'

The position seemed to be that Washington was initially prepared to abandon Gorbachov for the 'reformist' Yanayev, but was unwilling to do the same in favour of Boris Yeltsin. The White House had had a long history of dislike for Yeltsin: he had been snubbed on a visit to Washington in 1989; and when he returned to the US in June 1991, it was officially at the invitation of Senate leaders, not as the guest of the President. Bush felt that if he supported Yeltsin, he would undermine Gorbachov. In American eyes, Gorbachov represented stability in the Soviet Union: the Americans considered him to speak for the country as a whole, and he was therefore someone they could recognize and negotiate with. Despite being democratically elected by millions and despite his support for Western political values, Yeltsin was seen as a disruptive influence, favouring the dissolution of the Union and therefore making it much harder for Washington to deal with.

The outcome of the coup, and Yeltsin's eclipse of Gorbachov, made things difficult for Washington. The administration, of course, made haste to court the new man in power, but it showed itself to be deeply concerned by the precipitate break-up of the USSR. This was exactly what Washington's support for Gorbachov had been intended to avert. Just three weeks before the coup, Bush had made a strongly anti-separatist speech on a visit to Kiev, suggesting that allowing the USSR to fall apart could result in dangerous chaos. In making his remarks, Bush clearly had American interests at heart, and in the aftermath of August, those interests were being increasingly threatened.

The main concern of the White House was the fate of the Soviet Union's arsenal of nuclear weapons. While these were under the control of the 'reliable' central command of Gorbachov, America had felt they could be kept safe and eventually negotiated away. In the new conditions affecting the Soviet Union, the danger was that the missiles would fall into the hands of unpredictable leaders in newly independent republics. Already, during the confusion of the coup, the Kremlin's 'nuclear briefcase', which contains the codes needed to launch a nuclear attack, and which is supposed to stay always at the President's side, had disappeared for several hours. The situation had eventually been rescued by switching the launch control procedures to 'manual' (in other words, a nuclear strike would have had to be individually agreed by the three commanders of the armed forces: Shaposhnikov for the air force, Chernavin for the navy and Maksimov for the strategic rocket forces). But the precedent was worrying, and Boris Yeltsin was quick to play on the fear it had aroused in the Americans.

In the days after the coup, Yeltsin demanded that he as Russian President should have joint control with Soviet President Gorbachov, of the nuclear launch capability, and he announced that nuclear weapons currently stationed on Ukrainian territory would be withdrawn to Russia 'for security reasons'. He was making his claim to a place in the nuclear stakes, and to the international influence that goes along with it. George Bush was evidently concerned. At the end of September he proposed unprecedented reductions in Soviet and American nuclear weapons stocks, including the destruction of all short-range missiles, and much deeper cuts in long-range forces than had previously been considered possible. His offer, of course, was made to Mikhail Gorbachov; Yeltsin was 'consulted', but it was the Soviet President to whom the White House was

instinctively looking. The underlying suggestion was that Bush
wanted guarantees on the future safety of the Soviet arsenal before
the only man he trusted to give those guarantees was swept from
power.

While America's chief concern in the post-Communist era was
clearly military, Europe had economic considerations to worry
about too. At the G7 summit in London in July, the Soviets had
used the threat of their country's disintegration, and the economic
chaos that it would wreak on the rest of the world, as an argument
to win Western aid and trade credits. After August that threat looked
on the point of being fulfilled, and the spectre of a collapsing
Soviet Union sending millions of economic refugees westwards
into Europe seemed real. The countries whose geographical position
made them most vulnerable reacted with the greatest enthusiasm for
a prophylactic injection of Western capital into the USSR: Germany
proposed immediate aid, but other west European leaders repeated
the non-committal approach they had shown at the G7 meeting.

By the autumn of 1991 the Soviet leadership was appealing for
billions of dollars in Western help. Moscow was clearly counting on
the shock of the coup – and the fear of it happening again – to push
the world into a little self-interested generosity. The Soviets were also
removing the diplomatic obstacles which the West had previously
cited as standing in the way of economic assistance: the independence
of the Baltic states was formally recognized; a withdrawal of Soviet
troops from Cuba was announced; and an agreement was reached
with Washington to end all arms supplies to the warring factions
in Afghanistan. For the Japanese, there was a promise to speed up
the return of the disputed Kurile Islands, which had been seized by
the Soviet Union at the end of World War Two: in exchange, it was
suggested that Japan might provide fifteen billion dollars in urgent
economic aid.

The extraordinary changes within the Soviet Union had posed a
challenge for the world community. It was self-evidently in the common interest for the dismantling of the old USSR to be carried out
as calmly as possible. The country had moved into uncharted waters,
and more upheavals were still not ruled out: Eduard Shevardnadze,
the prophet of the first coup, was warning that another putsch could
still happen. The West's responsibility had become to support the
forces of reform in the new states; to provide necessary assistance
to those who would fight to avert a repetition of the August events;
and to take an active role in keeping the processes of change there

within the bounds of peaceful co-existence. The decisions taken by the West in response to the August events in the Soviet Union have the potential to determine whether a former adversary will develop into a future ally.

The collapse of Communism as a force in the international arena was the key political moment of the late twentieth century. The process of change since the dawning of perestroika has been rapid, and the precipitate rush into the future has made it a thankless task to attempt any considered stock-taking of the contemporary Soviet Union: further dramas tended to change the picture almost daily. But the death of Soviet Communism and the collapse of the Russian empire are epochal transformations which provide a rare chance to draw breath, and to place a comma if not a full stop at the end of an historical era. Gorbachov was right: we have entered a 'different world'.